More Praise for *The Good Among the Great*

"I have often puzzled over what it is that distinguishes people I admire for their character as well as their success. In *The Good Among the Great,* Donald Van de Mark gave me a framework to unlock this mystery, through insights into characters as strong and varied as Abraham Lincoln, Andy Grove, and Meryl Streep. The book is a thought-provoking, entertaining, and insightful guide to what makes special people truly special."

—James G. Coulter, cofounder, TPG

"Van de Mark makes the case for a deeper level of fulfillment, extracting insights from people famous and unknown, wealthy and modest, unique, quirky, and accomplished—all of them content. His book uncovers answers we all seek on reaching our peak potential and happiness. I read a lot of books on personal development; Van de Mark's approach stands out as one that combines clever observation with inspiration."

—Jory Des Jardins, cofounder, BlogHer

"Van de Mark has produced a great read in all senses of the word. *The Good Among the Great* is fun and takes you along for a look into a variety of famous people and, in so doing, gives you a much better read into yourself."

—Lawrence Lindsey, former Governor, Federal
Reserve System, and former Director, National
Economic Council

"With *The Good Among the Great*, Donald Van de Mark has created a deft synthesis of ideas ranging from thinkers such as Abraham Maslow and Joseph Campbell to business titans such as Warren Buffet and Jack Welch. In this truly useful guide for succeeding in the right way, Donald's keen insights as a journalist, entrepreneur, and businessman make him uniquely able to articulate his deeply humanistic messages in upbeat and constructive ways. This is a must-read for every person with serious ambition; it is a guide to a better way of succeeding in one's life and finding joy, solace, and pride in the simple act of doing. Van de Mark teaches all of us how to be better, more effective people and, ultimately, how to lead better lives."

—JOHN FISHER, cofounder, Draper, Fisher, Jurvetson

"*The Good Among the Great* explores how one can achieve simple success while at work or at play. Do unto others as you wish they would do unto you! You, too, will be full of love and life, and others will thank you for being good and great."

—ELSIE HILLMAN, philanthropist and Vice Chair, University of Pittsburgh Cancer Institute

Preface

I WAS A NEWSMAN. Like all news people, I had a beat— a territory I covered. Mine was people who are megasuccessful.

I've interviewed hundreds of leaders on the national and international scene, individuals who have reached "the top of the top" in fields ranging from business and politics to medicine and the performing arts. I've profiled polar explorers and business titans, politicians and popular authors, everyone from holistic medicine pioneer Andrew Weil to "CEO of the Century" Jack Welch.

Everybody knows what these people have accomplished; there's no news there. What I did was find out how they think and make choices so that I can decipher how their minds and hearts work, how and why they are so successful.

After more than twenty years of studying the best and most celebrated, I've learned that not all of these newsmakers are exemplary human beings. Most are okay; many are obsessed and ruthless, and some are even miserable. Many are feared, if not hated—not only by their competitors but also by their associates and staffs. They care little about the plight of others and the world at large.

Among the world's megasuccesses, however, is another group. This small minority is exceedingly aware, egalitarian, empathic, decent, and happy. Their associates and staffs love them; their competitors respect them. These people care deeply about others and often use their positions to help the larger community.

The high achievers who are also great human beings are part of an elusive subset. They usually don't seek the limelight, even though they're often in it. Unlike the fleeting success of many celebrities, their achievements endure as the world changes. They are often immensely successful, but their goals and achievements are usually beyond "success" narrowly defined. These people are the good among the great, and as different as they each are, they share certain personality traits.

While interviewing a series of Silicon Valley entrepreneurs, I heard similar attitudes and began to recognize patterns of behavior. I often heard variations of the same comments about what motivates them, how they think and behave, why they do what they do, why they don't make common mistakes, and why they often forfeit short-term gains. I began listing personality traits and private strategies that I heard echoed by all these "good guys." It reminded me of what Tolstoy wrote: "All happy families resemble one another, but each unhappy family is unhappy in its own way."[1] The good, grounded, big-hearted people resembled each other, and they were happy to tell me how they got that way.

I also realized that big-name successes aren't the only ones that belong in this select group. These prominent characters reminded me of some of the best people I've known since childhood. Some of my lifelong acquaintances, particularly from one summer colony on a beautiful lake in Canada, are also remarkably successful. But most of them lead quiet, private lives. You probably know some wonderful, uncelebrated characters too. I'm lucky enough to have known several families who seem to hand down good, strong personality traits from generation to generation. These families rear sweet children, responsible teenagers, and capable, wise adults. They often run important organizations while heading their own rambunctious families. A number are making new fortunes as well.

This book is about the hows and whys of admirable, creative and joyous people, with true stories about them and the personality traits that make them so. If you're looking for a step-by-step outline of how to make your first million, look elsewhere. If you're looking for a guide to being in service to others, creative, joyous, *and* materially successful, read on. Being a big winner in life isn't just about making money or even just accomplishing your goals.

As I share the following true stories, I'll draw upon the wisdom of the late, great twentieth-century psychologist Abraham Maslow. Often known as the father of positive psychology, Maslow is best known for his hierarchy of human needs. What most people don't know about Maslow is that he also studied those who keep evolving beyond their own needs.

In his later years, Maslow studied peak human beings—those whom he called "self-actualizing" individuals—a group he believed made up just 1 percent of the general population. Unfortunately, his theories on what made these people exceptional never made their way into popular parlance. But he did outline nineteen specific personality traits. In my interviews with the super-successful, I found that the dominant personality characteristics of the true-blue, good minority were very similar to the nineteen traits Maslow identified. This book in many ways proves Maslow's thinking. Maslow's seminal work, plus ideas from former U.S. Senator Bill Bradley, Professor Joseph Campbell, Rev. R. Maurice Boyd, Dr. Andrew Weil, and many others provide the theoretical and philosophical underpinnings for this book, which is divided into nineteen chapters, one per trait.

The book is also organized into four parts. Part 1 focuses on the development of a whole, true self and the traits that pertain to being an autonomous, ethical, and loving individual. This section is particularly relevant to children. We look at ways you can resist the zeitgeist, gain some detachment from your own thoughts, and prize your solitude.

In part 2 the focus is outward. The organizing principle for this section is "assessing the world clearly and efficiently." I'll share stories of how great people better understand others and events, so much so that they're often prescient about the future. These individuals are open to new experiences and have a sense of calm, even when faced with risk and the unknown. We'll also examine how the best human beings are not just interested in their own performance or results; they also "delight in the doing."

In part 3 you'll learn how strong, happy individuals care about and interact with others. For many reasons, these souls are egalitarian, have high empathy for others, and feel duty-bound to work for the benefit of all.

Part 4 outlines your personal payoff when you develop these personality traits: you can be more creative and more appreciative of your day-to-day life as well as more spontaneous, expressive, and joyful. We'll look at the histories of several admirable individuals and their propensity to have more transcendent, even mystical moments, or what Maslow called "peak" experiences, than the rest of us.

I wrote this book because I feel compelled to report an overarching conclusion—that there is a list of traits that we can identify in the good among the great and that most of us can develop these traits within ourselves. Personal evolution doesn't happen overnight and the most effective way to become a better, stronger human being is to surround yourself with healthy personalities. The first step in bringing these good souls into your orbit is knowing whom and what to look for, and that's where this book comes in.

Finally, in an age racked with catastrophes born of greed and self-aggrandizement, finding and promoting leaders who are fundamentally good people may be critical to preserving free markets and individual liberty and promoting good governance globally.

Introduction

It's better to hang out with people better than you. Pick out associates whose behavior is better than yours and you'll drift in that direction.

—WARREN E. BUFFETT

THIS BOOK IS FOR those of us given at least half a chance at life—meaning we've been blessed with enough love from our parents and enough success socially and professionally that we have some faith in our own ability to make ourselves, our lives, and the lives of those around us better.

These ideas are not for the cynical. Cynics won't believe that the stories here are true or that people of such high quality and noble intentions exist. And even if these cynics do believe that some mega-achievers can be genuinely good, they will doubt that a reader can adopt these attitudes and behaviors to improve his or her own future. The truth is that every story in this book is factual. Even if a name and details have been changed to protect someone's privacy, the facts and circumstances are real. And I know that people can change the trajectory of their lives because I have. I believe strongly that I was able to do so specifically because of habits and attitudes I adopted from a series of friends, family members, and leaders, several of whom are profiled in these pages.

Ever since I was a boy, I watched my favorite friends and their families and wondered how it is that some people, indeed some families, excel while others founder. I was fascinated by the fact that two talented people given virtually the same opportunities often ended up with starkly different results.

Then as a reporter I was intrigued that a few of the giants of our time were actually some of the nicest people I'd ever met. And I also saw that as many of my friends climbed to the highest rungs of society, they maintained their humanity and humility. These individuals remain grounded, true to themselves, and loyal to the people they've known. As busy as they are, they also use some of their precious time and a lot of their ample resources to reach out and help the wider community.

So this book is for people who want more—not just power, fortune, and fame, but awareness, experience, and fulfillment.

Through individual stories and examples, this book aims to explain how and why the people you admire are as good and happy as they are strong and capable. It will help you spot nineteen specific personality traits that the best human beings have and will give you some pointers about how to develop these traits within yourself. These pointers are condensed as "Takeaways" at the end of each chapter.

Feel free to jump into any chapter that intrigues you. The book is laid out with a certain progression in mind, but each chapter is also written to stand alone. For example, if you're particularly interested in what makes for earthbound success (money, power, and fame), then start with chapter 8, "Don't Kid Yourself." If you're interested in how those with the strongest temperaments find and foster lasting love, then go to chapter 2, "Have Lasting Love."

Also, each trait supports and even stimulates other traits. For instance, being more open to experience makes one appreciate the means as well as the ends. Being experiential also makes one a better perceiver of reality. So, you can start with the trait that you want to develop, and it will assist you in developing virtually all other eighteen.

Now a disclaimer: I'm not a psychologist and this text isn't meant to be a research paper or a psychological tome. It's meant to be understood and perhaps even enjoyed by a broad audience.

What I am is a trained observer of many of the most successful individuals of our time. As different as all of these characters are, you'll notice that several of them appear in more than one chapter. That's because they are among the fortunate few who exhibit most if not all of the traits we're looking at here. Returning to the same personalities helps us understand how the traits flow into and support each other.

There are nineteen traits and thus nineteen chapters, each with a principal story about someone who embodies that trait. The epilogue focuses on a person who, from all indications, has exhibited all the traits for many years—Meryl Streep.

You may already be asking, Aren't some lucky people simply *born* with strong, calm, and caring temperaments? Or maybe their parents taught them to be that way? Can only parents teach these traits to their own children? Maybe only impressionable children can learn them.

This takes us to the old "nature versus nurture" debate—and I come down squarely on both sides. Indeed, I come down on a third side as well. Yes, I believe that your genes matter. And yes, I also believe that you can learn better attitudes and behavior as a child. In fact, I *know* you can because I did.

But I also believe, as Dr. Stephen R. Covey teaches, that we are not just a product of nature or nurture, we are a product of choice, millions of choices that we make throughout our lives.[1] I believe that virtually all of us can learn the hows and whys of making better, smarter, more aware choices and in so doing have better lives and become better citizens.

I'm a reporter, and more specifically for this book, I feel like a messenger. And the message is this: some personality traits make people stronger and better. You can spot them in others and develop them within yourself.

So, read on and find ways to improve the way you perceive yourself and others. You may also become more caring and creative. Finally, you just might get back some of the joy and appreciation for life that you had as a wide-eyed youngster.

Part 1

Developing a True, Whole Self

....

Chapter 1

Be Uniquely You

TRAIT: *AUTONOMOUS*

It takes courage to grow up and become who you really are. The privilege of a lifetime is being who you are.

—E.E. CUMMINGS

BEST-SELLING AUTHOR AND HOLISTIC medicine pioneer Andrew Weil lives in Tucson, Arizona. But he didn't plan his life that way. Weil lives in Tucson simply because that's where his car broke down in the early 1980s, and he liked the place.

Because he was driving a Land Rover at the time, and no local repair shop had parts for the British SUV, Weil had to wait. He was stuck for more than a week and decided to relax and explore. Long before "snowbirds" and canyon ranchers invaded the region, this Philadelphia native embraced the desert with its dry air, distant vistas, and brilliant light. And at the end of a few days, the small voice in Weil's heart said simply, "This suits me." He responded by moving his whole life to Tucson—a choice that most of us would never dare make.

So many people, chief among them high-achieving Americans, don't do what's easiest. Even more surprising, they don't have the self-confidence to follow their deepest desires.

It's ironic, isn't it? We push ourselves to satisfy so many wants and expectations of others: spouses, clients, customers, bosses, children, and parents, and yet we postpone, ignore, and even dismiss our own quiet longings. If we're even aware of denied dreams, we often convince ourselves that we're exerting a kind of noble self-discipline, even a daily martyrdom. However we see the situation, a lot of us simply don't allow ourselves the kind of self-affirming choice that Andrew Weil made that week in Arizona and it costs us dearly.

In 2001, I interviewed Andrew Weil on his sprawling ranch just outside Tucson. One of the questions I asked was about the lucky breakdown and how a lot of us don't pick up on the opportunities that are presented to us. "What if you ignore these subtle signals?" I asked. "The same thing will keep coming up for you until either you do or you don't," he replied. "I tend to follow those clues from the universe. There is synchronicity in events, and the more one is tuned in to that, the more you can take advantage of those opportunities, be happier, and be guided along the path that will lead to greater freedom and greater usefulness."[1]

Clues from the universe? Freedom? Usefulness? What a way to explain the inexplicable twists and turns, and yes, car troubles of life! Weil is basically saying that we are not selfish to follow our wants. Instead, responding to your heart's desires can mean freedom for yourself and usefulness to others. These are lofty goals, not self-serving ones. You owe it to yourself and to the world to *be* yourself. The trick, of course, is to discover how.

In this chapter we're going to learn how and why the good among the great are first and foremost independent, self-directed, autonomous animals. We'll see how they know who they are and thus have a much calmer, more intuitive sense of who they are and where they're headed. There is an old expression, "If you don't know where you're going, then any road will take you there." In other words, many of us simply wander through time, disappointed that we don't reach certain destinations. If you don't start with self-awareness, which is a foundation for self-confidence, then you can't possibly have a strong hand in guiding your own destiny. Unless you are very talented and focused, you'll struggle to achieve anything of significance because you won't have refined and defined who you are and thus what you're best suited to pursue.

Maslow's Take

A lot of us need insightful, fearless friends to help us know ourselves and some of us may even need professional counsel. Here is a theoretical primer on the importance of personal autonomy and a description of how the best human beings live it.

First, the theory: Abraham Maslow, the twentieth-century psychologist who is best known for his hierarchy of human needs, called the psychologically healthiest and strongest individuals "self-actualizing." And he wrote that they "accept themselves and their own nature without chagrin or complaint or, for that matter, even without thinking about the matter very much."[2] These individuals don't wonder and certainly don't talk much about who they are and what they want. They just are, have no qualms about it, and go about satisfying their desires and reaching their goals. They're living their own, very distinctive, self-directed lives. And they come across as comfortable in their own skins.

Being autonomous or self-directed is not just a psychological state of mind, it's a fundamental tenet of American philosophy. Ralph Waldo Emerson celebrated it. William James lauds Emerson's emancipating creed, "Man has but to obey himself—He who will rest in what he is, is part of Destiny."[3]

One great way to spot individuals who are on their own paths, says Maslow, is "their relative independence of the physical and social environment."[4] In other words, they're not copycats or followers. And they certainly don't worry about what others think about them.

I've found that the autonomous usually had parents who are so supportive they've never had much reason to doubt themselves or their goals. They often come from happy, successful families and absorbed the confidence that comes from that. And if they do not come from happy families, they are distinctly autonomous from their relatives. Not that they don't care about their blood kin. They've sifted through and digested their childhood wounds and deprivations. Simply put, they don't let their pasts mar their current lives or future goals.

They're rarely insecure about their appearance, behavior, or life choices. To the rest of us, they seem assured, independent, and even sometimes detached or aloof. Maslow described them as "self-contained."[5] Another way to describe them is self-sufficient. They don't depend on approval from those around them. Indeed, they rarely depend on anyone but themselves. And they often don't subscribe to the norms and fashions to which most adhere (more on this in chapter 4).

Because they're very much characters of their own creation, they are typically very distinct people. They can, at times, come across as unusual if not a bit eccentric. Warren Buffett says this of his partner in business, Charlie Munger, "I would say everything about Charlie is unusual. I've been looking for the usual now for forty years, and I have yet to find it. Charlie marches to his own music, and it's music like virtually no one else is listening to."[6]

This doesn't mean that the best among us don't subscribe to society's norms. They typically do, but only as a way of not making waves, of avoiding unwanted attention from the conformity police among the rest of us.

How Can You Become More Autonomous?

To become more autonomous, first you have to accept your animal nature. The autonomous may be cool and comfortable about who they are, but they are definitely exuberant in their physical wants. Maslow writes, "The first and most obvious level of acceptance is at the so-called animal level . . . hearty in their appetites and enjoying themselves without regret or shame or apology."[7]

In other words these people tend to be good eaters, partiers, sleepers, competitors, laughers, and lovers! I've found that virtually all of them are keenly receptive to their senses. They are also sensual and have none if any of the shame that many of us have regarding sex.

This group fully accepts the nature of humankind in general, farts and all. You may think that you just read a typo. You didn't.

You can and *ought* to enjoy your animal instincts and acts, even bodily excretions. As one of my best friends (who honks loudly when he blows his nose) happily notes, "Expulsion from all orifices is pleasurable!"

Another friend, Robert Cunningham, once photocopied and distributed an obscure medical magazine piece about how breaking wind frequently and forcefully is a sign of good intestinal health. The gist of the article was that producing and pushing gas is quite natural and necessary and that a diet that produces plenty of gas is healthy, whereas eating overly processed foods and holding gas in is unhealthy. I was a teenager at the time and loved the article; I still do. I especially loved the fact that a pillar of the community distributed this important information to many a shocked matron.

Not all of us appreciate news on health such as this. Once on *Oprah*, a nutritionist said that a diet full of bran and other raw fruits and vegetables creates a lot of gas and that this was healthy. Winfrey wrinkled her nose a bit when she could have laughed with glee.

One other note about our physical natures: in a world of labor-saving devices, the good among the great are invariably exercisers. They revel in movement and exertion, knowing literally in their bones that moving blood around the body sets off a cascade of reactions that boost health, happiness, and longevity. They're often fierce competitors and love to win. Remember, these are strong people.

And because they are dedicated realists (chapter 8), they also recognize the flip side of pleasure. They know that our animal nature can be painful, dark, and even dangerous. However, unlike many realists who end up being fearful or fear mongers, they don't fret about it. They approach the subject with what Maslow called, "the stoic style . . . They can take the frailties and sins, weaknesses, and evils of human nature in the same unquestioning spirit with which one accepts the characteristics of nature . . . nature as it is and not as they would prefer it to be."[8]

For most of us, self-acceptance and autonomy also require that we take a moral inventory of our past poor behavior. This can be hard and painful work. For our purposes here, I can only offer this one bit of guidance: treat your own shameful acts with "tender contempt."

I once helped push a staff member of a little country club into the lake at a private party where she was an outsider and painfully aware of her lack of social status. She cried while she begged my stepcousin and me to let her go. We didn't. And no matter how much time has passed, I look back on that incident with deep shame and remorse.

Accepting your as well as humankind's, universal propensity for evil is helpful when coming to terms with your own failings. When you review your shameful acts, it's comforting to remember how natural bad behavior is, to think how much worse others have behaved, and to try to make things right with those you've wronged. In addition to these techniques, it's helpful to grasp a bit of grace and forgive yourself. As the late Reverend R. Maurice Boyd used to counsel at the City Church of New York, "Look back on your own transgressions in life with 'tender contempt.'"[9] Don't feel any less disgust at your behavior—just treat yourself gently. You are not perfect. If you treat your own transgressions with tenderness, you'll be better able to treat others' with tenderness too.

Another Individual Who Is Autonomous

Jim Barksdale is a business icon of the 1980s and 1990s. He was at the helm of FedEx as the company virtually created the overnight delivery business. Then he was CEO of the first popular Web browser, Netscape.

In 2000, during an interview for *Nightly Business Report*, I asked Barksdale this question: "Should the *ambitious* person go where the best job opportunities are or live where he or she most wants to live and find the best opportunity there?"

His answer was immediate and unequivocal: "There are great jobs everywhere! First start out, 'What's going to make you happy?' Now everybody is not as family-oriented as I am. I love to be around our children and my wife. So first let's establish an environment that we would enjoy, around people we enjoy. We have the talent and ability and the wherewithal to do most of these things, and there are great jobs everywhere, so let's *then* decide what we are going to do."[10]

Do you hear the confidence and joy in Barksdale's philosophy of life and work? "First let's establish an environment that we would enjoy, around people we enjoy." Note that I specifically emphasized to Barksdale that I was asking about what an *ambitious* person ought to do. His answer was still, "First, start out, 'What's going to make you happy?'" Hallelujah!

Moving or changing jobs with all the unknowns is scary and usually hard work. If you want to shake up your life in some profound way and find that you're frozen, unable to make the moves that you want or need, just keep in mind that by their very nature, *transitions are temporary.* Changing cities, jobs, and whole careers is uncomfortable, but only for a year or so. Once you've been through one calendar of seasons, deadlines, and holidays, you'll have a foundation of friends, habits, and skills on which to build your preferred existence.

Good people and good jobs are everywhere—don't worry about that. Worry about what the late, great professor of comparative religion Joseph Campbell said: "I think the person who takes a job in order to live—that is to say, for the money—has turned himself into a slave."[11]

Jack Welch also pushed the notion that you ought to do what makes you happy. This is what he said to me in 2001 when he was still CEO of General Electric: "This is where you spend your life! Have a ball at it. Why would you want to come to a place as a stuffed shirt and hang around a corporation? It's dumb, unless you had a ball at it!"[12]

Of course, Welch could be a very tough taskmaster. But if you were good at your job, and even more so, if you were good and enthusiastic about your work, he was your biggest supporter.

Bill Bradley, the former basketball star and U.S. senator from New Jersey, once encapsulated this whole notion with this statement, "The externals of one's life ought to reflect the internals. You have to live your life not to the drumbeat of others' expectations. You have to live your life to the drumbeat of your inner self."[13]

Bradley is wiser and more philosophical than most leaders, meaning he cares about the whys of life as much as the hows, whens, and wheres. He asks himself and urges others to ask, "Why am I alive? What am I doing?"

If this sounds a little too New Age for you, remember that discovering who you are and crafting an autonomous life is an *ancient* human pursuit. "Who am I?" is the oldest question in philosophy. Some of the greatest expressions of human wonder dwell on self-awareness and self-fulfillment: "An unexamined life is not worth living," "Know thyself," or as Friedrich Nietzsche exhorted us all, "Become what Thou art!"[14]

William James then raises the stakes by tying self-awareness and self-determination with character. But he also gives us an emotional signpost that we can each look for to know the moments when we find that which is the "real" self. In June 1887 James wrote his fiancée, Alice Gibbens, "the best way to define a man's character would be to seek out the particular mental or moral attitude, in which . . . he felt himself most deeply and intensely active and alive. At such moments there is a voice inside which speaks and says 'this is the real me.'"[15] Note that it is not to excel or to win on the one hand and to "Be kind" or to "Think globally and act locally" on the other. Every human being's goal is the same (though, when applied, wonderfully different): be yourself as thoroughly, consistently, and honestly as you can. Or like the tagline for the U.S. Army, "Be all you can be."

Figuring out what you want and ought to do will require preparation, experimentation, and support from those in your life. And, yes, once you know what it is that you want and are meant to do, you will have to muster great intestinal fortitude to pursue it. But recognize that acting on the right choices is one definition of wisdom. According to the *Shorter Oxford English Dictionary*, the wise don't just know the right choice; they make that choice as a "habitual manner of action."[16]

But no matter how much bravery it may take, making the right choice should never require sacrificing yourself. If you are a high-achieving, Six Sigma, *7 Habits of Highly Effective People* person whose daily routine is now a chore or a bore, you may happily jettison one of your long-held beliefs: that self-sacrifice is necessary to achieve your goals.

If you have postponed your wants, your dreams, and yourself every day in some job or pursuit that you no longer love (if you ever loved it in the first place), the time has come to do what you truly want and are meant to do. And not just because you've earned it, but because you will achieve far more for yourself and, very likely, for others.

Maslow described this as a "healthy selfishness, a great self-respect, a disinclination to make sacrifices without good reason."[17]

Many of the nastiest people among the high achievers I've interviewed don't understand this. Usually, they're punishing the people around them as they push themselves. But the good among the great insist that pushing yourself through years of drudgery or working for screaming bullies is more of a hindrance than a help to your upward and outward trajectory.

If your routine is drudgery, if you're afraid or feel exhausted, then you are not on your path. If you really think about it, it's not even your life. And how can you possibly succeed more at a life that's not of your choosing than one that is?

You may be thinking, "This guy doesn't understand how competitive my life is!"

I *do* know how competitive it is. I went to some of the most competitive schools, wormed my way into and then worked my way up in the television news business when everyone's son and daughter wanted to be Peter Jennings and Jane Pauley. Then I helped launch a Web site and television production company in the hypercompetitive dot-com boom. One thing I'm sure of—it's far tougher to compete successfully when you're not excited by what you do.

Living a daily routine where the externals of your life reflect the internals is not easy. In fact, you're probably going to have to be *more* sensitive, *more* creative, *more* flexible, and certainly *more* courageous to live that life than if you simply soldier on in the name of providing for your family or maintaining your social status. But the critical thing is it's going to be *your* life. You will have ten times more joy and are likely to be more successful as a result.

Having been a business and finance reporter, I know full well that earthly autonomy means financial independence too. The good among the great that I've known usually make plenty of money. At least, they make more than enough to be independent. And if they've been given cash, they're thrifty savers. Even the richest are often frugal—Costco millionaires. They've often worked very hard for their money and consider wasting it foolish, even sinful. They see savings as a proxy for freedom and as security against disaster. They use their money for education and travel—more education about the earth and other cultures. They give a lot of it away.

If they've grown up around money, they tend to not spend much on expensive material goods. And most of them know that the psychic pleasure derived from fancy cars, clothes, and houses is fleeting.

No one can tell another person how to live an autonomous life. It's up to you to march to your own drumbeat, not to that of others. And if you're still apprehensive about making a major shift, make some small ones and see how you feel. If the decision lightens your heart, keep moving in that direction. You'll be applying your smarts, skills, accumulated wisdom, and newly discovered drive to work that propels you out of bed in the morning. If you've been successful in an occupation that doesn't excite you, how can you fail in one that does? We'll discuss much more on the specific subject of means and ends in chapter 10.

Choosing to live a daily existence that you love is so compelling a message that advertisers use it all the time. In December 2009, BlackBerry's tagline was "Do what you love. Love what you do." The good among the great individuals whom I've interviewed have no problem feeling, knowing, and accepting who they are and then constructing lives that match their wants and needs. It makes them better leaders because their exuberance excites others. Because they are thoroughly true to themselves, they are more integrated and thus authentic. They are appreciative of the need for those around them to follow their own specific and evolving paths and this appreciation attracts and keeps talent, giving their success greater longevity.

Another Autonomous Person

Most of us struggle at least a bit to know and accept ourselves, and we struggle a lot to create autonomous lives that reflect our true selves. Of course, some people are born into and reared in temperamentally strong, sensitive, and endlessly supportive families. Perhaps it's in their DNA to be self-accepting and internally guided. Autonomy is typically a big part of their upbringing, so it naturally becomes part of their conscious philosophy of life.

As a result they have the kind of experiences my friend Jim Armstrong had when he was fifteen years old. On one of his first days at Andover, a boarding school in Massachusetts, he headed out of his dorm and he stopped to breathe in the crisp air of a fall morning. Then, from around the corner of the gym, came the sight and sound of the varsity football team. In high spirits, the squad jogged past him and out onto a playing field. Jim remembers them barking some rah-rah chant as they went through early morning calisthenics. Gangly, bespectacled, and musical, Jim watched as the jocks counted out their exercises.

At that moment, the realization struck Jim that that kind of boisterous, physical fellowship was not for him. Not that it was bad, silly, or unattainable; he simply had little interest in or need for it. In fact, Jim and his artistic pals created their own competition—about who could avoid sports longer, necessitating ever more elaborate infirmary excuses and harebrained schemes. Jim knew, even at that insecure age (and in high school, of all places!), who he was and who he was not. To this day, Jim thinks nothing of the self-assuredness he felt at that formative age.

Most teenagers don't know themselves very well and grope toward self-awareness, let alone self-acceptance. They're often pushed by parents into certain areas of study, activities, and sports. They can't help but doubt themselves. They often respond with passive resistance and experiment with wayward behavior, while those from the healthiest families get all the acceptance and respect that they need to know who they are. Thus the self-aware, self-affirmed teenagers are armed against all those tempters who would convince them otherwise.

Not recognizing who you are and not making the choices to fulfill your own destiny is a tragedy. It is a crime against nature—

your nature. It is a profound loss to you and all those around you. As far as philosophy goes, self-recognition is also a fundamental tenet of American thinking. No less than William James wrote, "All that the human heart wants is its chance."[18] Going through life missing who you are makes for a deathbed scene full of regrets and anguish over self-denial, unfulfilled dreams, and lost potential. Recognizing your true self, stepping forward as that person, evolving and thriving as you forge a daily path that is yours are your fundamental duties to yourself. Building a genuine life based on your unique potential is actually a lifelong series of options, large and small. The big ones are "moments of truth," your truth.

The Reverend R. Maurice Boyd's Take

Autonomous individuals have internalized what the late Reverend R. Maurice Boyd loved to declare: "Life is a *drama*, not a process." They recognize that they are protagonists and coauthors in lives of their own making. As a result, they give themselves both more freedom to enjoy life and more responsibility for their own happiness. They understand and accept that some of their destiny is out of their control—because of their DNA, their upbringing, or simply because of random chance. They may even ascribe some of life's perplexing twists and turns to God's will or interpret them as signals from the universe. But they also know and thrive in the belief that *much of their own lives is within their control*. They are not just actors on a stage. They are coauthors of their own dramas.

A protestant Irishman, Boyd made self-discovery and self-direction regular themes in his sermons at the City Church of New York. In July 1999, I interviewed him at New York's Society for Ethical Culture, where he said, "Literature is just full of all that stuff—of somehow having life but missing life. Lots of people feel like that about their own lives. They're still waiting to appear. They don't know who they are, what they're doing, or what it means, and very often they don't give any thought to that."[19]

Too many of us, warned Boyd, don't truly know ourselves and our true wants, and so we pursue unworthy goals. "What you want becomes your basic principle. What you're after will determine the nature of your 'gathering in.' And the terrible thing is people realize too late that many of the things that they're going after don't keep their promises. A perfect definition of Hell for me is to have everything you ever wanted and still be dissatisfied, still feel as if you've missed something."[20]

This self-reckoning is serious stuff, but it is also exhilarating stuff. Think of Ebenezer Scrooge, and how the spirits of Christmas past, present, and future force old Ebenezer to rethink all his values. And what about Harry Potter? In *Harry Potter and the Chamber of Secrets*, Professor Dumbledore counsels the young wizard, "It is our choices, Harry, that show what we truly are, far more than our abilities."[21]

Autonomy means looking within, accepting and acting on your deepest, truest desires, forging a life that reflects you, and then relaxing about it! Being autonomous is both harder and easier than most of us think. One truth is inescapable: The buck stops with you because an autonomous life starts with you.

If you are more yourself, lo and behold, a fantastic array of side effects happens. You are far more likely to be who you *ought* to be. You'll naturally be more serene, spontaneous, expressive, integrated, loving, jolly, and joyous—all traits of people Abraham Maslow called "self-actualizing" and traits that are covered in future chapters of this book.

We're back to the advice from the beginning of this chapter. If you're not one of the 1 percent who Maslow believed were the healthiest temperamentally, then you'll have to work a bit to get on your path to reach your potential.

As you do, remember these voices:

Andrew Weil: "Follow those clues from the universe, take advantage of those opportunities, be happier, and be guided along the path that will lead to greater freedom and greater usefulness."

Jim Barksdale: "First, start out with 'What's going to make you happy?'" (Make your happiness a means as well as an end.)

Bill Bradley: "The externals of one's life ought to reflect the internals." (Your heart and instincts will guide you as well as your thoughts.)

William James: "All that the human heart wants is its chance."

Jack Welch: "Have a ball!"[22]

Takeaways

Knowing who you are and forging a life that suits you are the most personal and exciting tasks you have as a human being. Unless and until you define who you are and who you aim to be, you are handicapped in achieving your great goals.

- ✓ Wake up to your daydreams and recognize the inner desires they illuminate.
- ✓ Be honest with yourself about your evolving needs, wants, likes, and dreams.
- ✓ Respect and feed your animal appetites—eat, love, carouse, and exercise. Just don't forget to hold yourself responsible for your instincts too.
- ✓ Plan and then make shifts so that you spend more time being where you want to be, working where and with whom you want to work, being with whom you want to be.
- ✓ Recognize and accept responsibility for your choices and your life as it is. Your daily routine moves you toward or away from being more authentically you as well as more productive and happier.
- ✓ Measure your choices as much by your inner values as by the world's outer or material values.
- ✓ Encourage others, especially children, to follow their dreams, large and small.

....

Chapter 2

Have Lasting Love

TRAIT: *LOVING*

*Being deeply loved by someone gives you
strength, while loving someone deeply gives you
courage.*

—LAO TZU

POOSIE ORR KNOWS ALL about love. She's been giving it and receiving it her whole life. Poosie's given name is actually Paula. She's called Poosie because as an infant, her mother carried her in a papoose.

The matriarch of a Pittsburgh family who vacations on the same lake in Canada as my family, Poosie is exceptional in her ability to love and connect with others. And she instilled that trait in her four children. How does she do it? In her own words, "You have to have a comfort about yourself so you can think about other people." That comfort comes from "you having enough . . . being *given* enough love so that you're not worried."[1]

For Poosie, the mother of four and grandmother of six, the ability to give and receive love starts in childhood. "The two lasting things parents can give to their children are roots and wings. The roots—that's the security, a kind of comfort about yourself. And if you're given that, then it's going to extend your curiosity and your interest in heaven knows what! And then you're given partly your wings—give it a whirl, give it a try."[2]

Nowhere is this philosophy better manifested than in Poosie's own parenting style. As a mom she made a point of "loving [her children] for what *they* wanted, hoping to help them follow what they wanted to do." Instead of imposing her personal set of goals and ideals on her children, she respected them enough to let them have their own. How different from the smothering, controlling love of so many "helicopter parents" today!

Take Poosie's eldest son as an example. David Orr lives in Hawaii and works as a conservationist. Hawaii is afflicted with a myriad of invasive plant species, so David runs an Audubon center on Oahu—a nonprofit garden enclave that protects native species. He doesn't make much money, and the house he lives in isn't much more than a shack.

And yet, when Poosie talks about "Davey," she does it in the most glowing terms because he's doing exactly what *he's* meant to do. "He loves his knowledge of growing things . . . and preserving them. He's a preserver, as well as an archaeologist, a conservationist. What he's doing is *important* in the world."[3]

Though he works for "a piddling amount . . . it doesn't bother him at all." Therefore, it doesn't bother Poosie. She understands that David doesn't need a bigger income because he's got no family to support and no tuition bills. He's incredibly fulfilled doing what he's doing, and as a result, Poosie is fulfilled. Her second son is entrepreneurial; currently he's building a potato-vodka brand called Boyd and Blair. Her third son is a consultant in Washington, DC, and her daughter "is teaching her heart out in Denver." They're all very different, each is thriving, and the latter three are married and raising happy youngsters of their own. So many parents, even good, capable parents, constrict the lives of their children, whether consciously or unconsciously. They're concerned about their needs or fears, about appearances, competition, or conforming to the status quo. Very often they are troubled by some wound that they themselves suffered long ago, and they now trouble their children with faulty coping mechanisms. As a result, the love they show their children comes with stipulations or conditions. These parents have endless rules about the way their children ought to act and think and even about what they should want.

Poosie and her husband, Charlie, raised their offspring quite differently. "We sure had fun loving them for what they wanted. Hoping to help them get to do what they wanted to do." Also, Charlie and Poosie imposed very few rules. "The only reason we have rules is that you want to keep them healthy. 'Get your shot if you need it . . . Don't ride your bicycle in the street if it's a highway'—you know, those kinds of things."[4]

Beyond health and safety, there was no *need* for rules and regulations. "You want them to have fun," Poosie said with a grin. "You want them to have fun! And to be able to do what they want to do. If you give your children enough love, they have a kind of security . . . an independence . . . a freedom."[5]

"Did your children ever let you down?" I asked. Poosie looked a little shocked by the question and then thought carefully. "No . . . No!" she declared. Poosie and Charlie were the kind of parents who barked a happy "Have fun!" as their (then) teenagers headed out anywhere. Virtually everything—school, work, travel—was supposed to be joyous.[6]

It is precisely this sense that life is to be enjoyed, not endured, that you have great choices in who you want and ought to be that gives strength to children and lays the groundwork for them to become outwardly focused adults who naturally have a lifelong ability to love others.

In this chapter we're going to see how the good among the great love and are loved. We'll see how deeply they share their affection and how careful they are in choosing whom they love. And we'll see how their autonomy of character allows them to overcome some of the paradoxes that flummox the rest of us in our love lives.

Maslow's Take

Abraham Maslow's findings on love—the third layer in his hierarchy of human needs—are about autonomy as much as they are about affection. "What we see in the love relationship," he writes, "is a fusion of great ability to love, and at the same time, great respect for the other."[7]

Poosie Orr has mastered this fusion in her philosophy as a mom. She has never invaded her children's personal space or crossed their boundaries—not when they were growing up, nor now when they are adults. Thus she has four very different and independent characters to track and love. When asked what she thinks of the current generation of parents who often hover over their offspring, she lamented, "Oh, it makes me cry! I can't think of anything worse than parents who go visit their kids at college four times a year. There you are, doing your own thing in college . . . that's when you're on your wings! Don't those parents have something else to do?"[8]

For Poosie, that situation is not about the children needing the parents; it's the parents needing their kids. "These parents are

crying to be needed. So they say, 'Oh, I've really got to go see baby
Jane, I know she misses me.' Oh, phhhhtt."[9]

According to Maslow, Poosie's right. Real love isn't dependent—it isn't mired in need or compulsion. Real love is *inter*dependent, allowing each person the fullest expression of themselves
free of need or demand.

This interdependence is mirrored in the context of romantic
relationships too. The fusion of love and respect "shows itself in
the fact that [exemplary] people cannot be said in the ordinary
sense of the word to 'need' each other, as do ordinary lovers. They
can be extremely close together, and yet go apart when necessary
without collapsing. They do not cling to each other, or have hooks
or anchors of any kind. One has the definite feeling that they
enjoy each other tremendously, but would take philosophically
a long separation or a death; that is, and would remain strong.
Throughout the most intense and ecstatic of love affairs, these
people remain themselves and remain ultimately masters of themselves as well, living by their own standards even though enjoying
each other intensely."[10]

What a far cry from how our culture portrays love! "True,
romantic love" is more often than not depicted as a desperate, tor-
mented, Romeo-and-Juliet affair. Thousands of songs and movies
and books come out every year devoted to love, and that kind of
love is almost always centered on the idea of need, heartbreak,
and pain.

In Maslow's opinion, healthy love needs to be redefined by
popular culture. What we've long thought of as a "complete merg-
ing of egos" is in fact two already complete egos, strengthening
each other in their individuality and assisting each other in reaching their full potential. In this way, two people become partners
and maintain their individual identities instead of losing their
separateness when they merge.

The idea is not just for lovers. A sense of autonomy for oneself and freedom for the beloved should characterize *any* relationship, whether it's between parent and child, siblings or friends, as well as lovers.

Gender Roles

Maslow also discovered that exceptionally healthy couples ignore cultural role models and make "no really sharp differentiation between the roles and personalities" of male and female. He goes on, "they did not assume the female was passive and the male active, whether in sex or love or anything else. These people were all so certain of their maleness and femaleness that they did not mind taking on some of the cultural aspects of the opposite sex role . . . It was especially noteworthy that they could be both active and passive lovers and this was clearest in the sexual act and in physical love-making. Kissing and being kissed, being above or below in the sexual act, taking the initiative, being quiet and receiving love, teasing and being teased—these were all found in both sexes."[11]

Another surprising finding by Maslow about love among those individuals with particularly healthy personalities is that not only do they not need others to love them, they typically select very few to whom they extend their love, and when they're not in love, they seem to need sex less than the rest of us.

The Obamas and the "No New Friends" Rule

In December of 2008, the *New York Times* ran the following headline: "Obama's Friends Form Strategy to Stay Close." The article, by Jodi Kantor, describes the particularly solid friendship of Barack and Michelle Obama and three couples closest to them.[12]

For over a decade, the group has strengthened their ties over Scrabble games, barbecues, vacations, and child-rearing. These close friends also became deeply involved in Obama's presidential campaign, acting in a variety of roles from informal advisors to traveling companions. As the Obamas prepared to move to the White House, all expressed some worry over how they would maintain the closeness they had shared.

Most striking, Kantor notes that "in the presidential campaign, the Obamas had a 'no new friends' rule, surrounding themselves with a coterie of familiar faces." This rule is classic of the good among the great. Because they have "especially deep ties with rather few individuals," Maslow writes that "their circle of friends is rather small. The ones that they love profoundly are few in number . . . Devotion is not a matter of a moment." For the psychologically healthiest among us, love is a very intense feeling, and sharing intimately can only possibly be done with a trusted few. If you think about it, no one has the time and energy to truly love more than a handful of people at any given point in his or her lifetime. When we consider that people with exceptionally strong temperaments self-select each other, it's no surprise that they purposely limit their deep affections to only a few.

They even use the word "love" warily because for them, love is such an intense and heartfelt commitment. As Maslow puts it, "They applied it to only a few rather than to many, tending to distinguish sharply between loving someone and liking the person or being friendly or benevolent or familial."[13] They're also very discriminating simply because building a communicative, loving, trusting relationship involves a commitment of significant time, energy, and effort. While Facebook may point to the contrary, no one can really have one thousand friends.

It is important to note here that a true friend is someone to whom you can confide your hopes, concerns, feelings, and fears. The majority of people we call friends are really acquaintances with whom we are friendly.

However, there is another paradox here—while deeply loving just a few, these individuals also have great affection for people in general. They tend to be kind to nearly everyone, children in particular.

More Individuals Who Are Loving: Rachel Walton and Resuscitating One's Heart

Mrs. John F. Walton, Jr. was a legend in the Pittsburgh community. She lived to be 107 years old before passing away in 2006 and was proud that she had lived in three centuries. Her husband passed away in 1974, when he was eighty-one. So Mrs. Walton, affectionately known as "Nan" to her prolific offspring (four children, sixteen grandchildren, and twenty-three great-grandchildren), and hundreds of others, lived for thirty-two years without her beloved "Jack."

While she missed him, she was quite content to go on. Rachel Walton, one of those grandchildren—(and her namesake) noted that "Nan did really well after Granddad died. She kept going. But she did carry a picture of him with her everywhere. She always had a picture out wherever she traveled. He was very much present for her. But she had charity work, a lot of friends, big family—a lot of involvements."[14]

As we learned in chapter 1, an autonomous personality fosters great strength even in the face of hard knocks. When she was just ninety-nine, I interviewed Nan and she lamented that "I haven't got one old friend left . . . Last year, my last one went." I asked if she was ever tempted to just give up or "fade away." She looked startled for a second and then declared, chuckling, "I don't go for fading away."[15]

The younger Rachel, who is a pediatric and hospice nurse, doesn't go for fading away either despite her own deep losses. She lost the love of her youth when after a ten-year romance, he chose another woman. "When that first love ended," she said, "I made a commitment to not be a bitter person. That has been one of those life 'resolves.' I kept opening my heart. I worked hard to stay open to work and friendship. Life has not been easy—there've been hard moments and strong losses. But I had this commitment to keep my heart open, in part because I saw others who did get bitter and closed down."[16]

One of the ironies of developing particularly good psychological health is that you feel more. Because you are more aware and more receptive, your feelings—joy and delight, empathy and agony are all more intense. You are also a better recognizer of reality and thus to the capriciousness and cruelty of life (more on this in chapter 8). If the cost of possessing strength and awareness is deeper pain, then its benefit is that you're able to withstand and move through it. Rachel did. She was "filled with jealousy toward this other woman." But instead of sublimating or medicating her pain away, Rachel faced and felt her feelings fully: "I let myself have my emotions. I cried; I was angry and did not pretend otherwise. I was so angry, hurt, and devastated—I could have gone to a very bad place. I could have shut down, become isolated, and become hard. I didn't want that. Part of it is just making that commitment, part of it through therapy, part of it through friendships—really opening up to others, being myself, showing people my vulnerability to have real relationships."[17]

At that excruciating time in her life, Rachel found relief by focusing outward, on others and by recognizing how much she still had. "I was working with teenagers at the time with cystic fibrosis . . . they would die in their teenage years. And there were times that you were around them as they struggled to catch their breath. It always offered me perspective."[18]

When asked now about love, Rachel admits, "It's very hard to stay open and loving and not have a place to put that love.

To not have someone respond to it . . . it can be very hard. But there are other places to focus it: work, animals, nature, art, being creative."[19]

We'll have more on focusing outward and on others in chapters 13 and 14, and more on recovering your creativity in chapter 16.

Maslow writes that superior psyches "live more in the real world of nature" than the rest of us.[20] After losing her first love, Rachel literally dwelled in nature. "I moved to New Mexico, spent a lot of time walking in those mountains, seeing beautiful things, smelling the air, seeing trees, seeing blue sky—very healing—and it kept me open."[21]

"Nature did that for you?" I asked.

"Being a little closer to the earth, to the elements, to the seasons, the rhythms, and seeing the *endurance.* It all endures. I don't know if it's conscious; looking at ancient trees and boulders, but I think being in the presence of that you get that message . . . and going outside in all the seasons, you see the never-ending cycle, life and death, rebirth, you get that information into yourself."[22]

At the age of fifty, Rachel married for the first time. She married a whole human being, just as she had grown to be. And her wedding was the most elegant and the most intimate I've ever witnessed. Elegance and intimacy—a rare combination.

Lucky in Love: The Role of Appreciation

When asked to describe her marriage to her late husband Charlie, Poosie Orr smiled and choked up a bit, "Pretty swell . . . pretty lucky . . . pretty lucky! He loved me, and I loved him . . . quite simple." Then she brightened, "And we had a lot of laughs!"[23]

Did they squabble? Did Poosie ever wonder if she'd made the right choice?

"Oh sure," she said. "Who doesn't? But that's the way it goes . . . very, very lucky."

In chapter 15, we'll take a much deeper dive into the trait of being appreciative. Poosie says that love very often springs from appreciation. When talking about our place on the lake, she said, "You wouldn't love it so much if you didn't appreciate it."[24]

But as we've learned, appreciation is only a part of the story. Love is about being autonomous and flexible in the relationship and remembering that it's not all about you and what you think the relationship ought to be or look like. "If you can try to be flexible, it's good," said Poosie. "It'll certainly make things a lot easier. You're going to be able to deal with things better if you don't have to do 'this, this, and this' at eight o'clock."[25]

In other words, love is not about pushing or forcing yourself, a partner, or the relationship to be a certain way. Maslow writes that those individuals in healthy relationships not only act with more spontaneity but also with "the dropping of defenses, the dropping of roles and of trying and striving in the relationship."[26]

"How about *aiming*?" Poosie suggested, "It's not about pushing. And then, if that aim, that star over there on the left, if you don't get there . . . well, maybe that star down on the right would be better. But, try to make it so you're able to change your course. But pushing? No. Pushing involves force and you don't want that."[27]

Maslow would agree. He makes it clear that to love and to be loved is not about forcing or even doing anything; the good among the great "no longer strive in the ordinary sense, but rather develop."[28] For the best human beings among us, giving and receiving love is about *being*, "It had better be said that they have the power to love and the ability to *be* loved."[29]

Takeaways

Healthy love does not subsume or suppress the individual. It supports and respects each person's autonomy.

✓ If you're a parent, show love by respecting your children. Avoid "helicopter parenting," and give them freedom as well as support.

✓ Avoid the word "should" when speaking with those you love. Giving directives and unsolicited advice is a sign that you are not giving your loved one his or her autonomy.

✓ Demonstrate rather than declare your love. Be careful when using the word "love." Reserve it for the few that you have the time, intensity, and commitment to truly love. Overuse can diminish its meaning.

✓ Be flexible and open to new goals if your and your loved one's ambitions are not met, separately or together.

✓ If you and your loved ones are not constantly evolving and discovering more about yourselves, then you may not be in healthy relationships.

....

Chapter 3

Be True-Blue

TRAIT: *ETHICAL*

*Always be ready to speak your mind, and a base
man will avoid you.*

—WILLIAM BLAKE

IN JANUARY 2002 EVERYONE was talking about an
accountant from Texas. This number cruncher never expected to
be a national celebrity, but suddenly, she was. And all because of
a letter.

Sherron Watkins grew up in Tomball, Texas, a suburb of
Houston. She was a sorority girl at the University of Texas at
Austin, where she earned two accounting degrees. After graduating, she worked first at Arthur Andersen before moving to an
energy-based company in Houston—America's seventh-largest
company, as a matter of fact—called Enron.

In less than a decade, Watkins rapidly climbed the ranks to become vice president of corporate development. But along the way, she started noticing that something was off. She'd always had a flair for numbers, and the numbers just weren't adding up.

It took her weeks to work up the nerve, but finally, in August 2001, Watkins sent a seven-page letter to her boss, Ken Lay, telling him what he already knew: that the company was essentially a well-disguised Ponzi scheme of epic proportions. She also voiced her concerns to a friend at Arthur Andersen, the firm responsible for auditing Enron.

"I am incredibly nervous that we will implode in a wave of accounting scandals," she wrote in her letter to Lay. "My eight years of Enron work history will be worth nothing on my resume, the business world will consider the past successes as nothing but an elaborate accounting hoax."[1]

She went on to say: "I have heard one manager-level employee from the principal investments group say, 'I know it would be devastating to all of us, but I wish we would get caught. We're such a crooked company.'"[2]

A few short months later, the jig was up: Enron stock plummeted and the company collapsed, filing for what was then the largest bankruptcy in history. The letter Watkins wrote ended up on the desks of criminal and congressional investigators, along with thousands of other documents illuminating Enron's shady dealings. Watkins made national headlines and earned the moniker that made her famous: the "Enron whistleblower."

In a 2009 interview with *Human Resource Executive,* Watkins described her life today as "extremely good." She's no longer at a desk from nine to five; she now works as a professional speaker on the corporate circuit "earning a full-time living for working part-time."[3]

Talking about her career change, Watkins said: "The media made me a hero. I was on the cover of *Time*. But your corporate career is dead. People decide you're more loyal to the truth than to the organization. Even those of us who [blew the whistle] internally never ended up working in the same field again."[4]

Loyalty to the truth set the stage for the defining moment of Watkins's professional career, and that loyalty is exactly what makes her a whole, integrated, and ethical individual—the third trait of self-actualizing human beings. It also catapulted her into a speaking career that she loves.

In this chapter, we're going to look at how and why the good among the great typically exhibit high integrity. We'll see that they have higher and more objective standards of behavior—especially for themselves. We'll also demonstrate why immoral behavior is so costly and moral behavior is so rewarding.

Maslow's Take

Maslow wrote in his book *Motivation and Personality* that the particularly strong, healthy personalities he studied "rarely showed in their day-to-day living the chaos, the confusion, the inconsistency, or the conflict that are so common in the average person's ethical dealings."[5] Thus, while corporate America still has a conflicted view over the propriety of Watkins's actions, she herself has and had no confusion about what was right and wrong.

In *The Farther Reaches of Human Nature*, Maslow goes on to write, "Self-actualization is an ongoing process. It means making each of the many single choices about whether to lie or be honest, whether to steal or not to steal . . . and it means to make each of these choices as a growth choice."[6]

In other words, self-actualization or true psychological health is not just about morals. It's about *growth*. The quality and clarity of your ongoing moral and ethical choices will determine how whole and integrated you become as a human being. If you compromise your ethical choices, you not only hurt others, you fracture your personality, which results in a variety of negative consequences.

People who are unethical have to compartmentalize their choices, their thinking and behavior. The true-blue among us understand and *relax* in the habit of making each choice part of a unified life of authenticity. In other words, they have the ability to integrate all the strands of their personality so that they can be true, not just to others and themselves, but to reality—the truth. Hence, Sherron Watkins's "loyalty to the truth" trumped the loyalty that others felt she should have had to "the organization." In spite of the grave threat that coming forward posed to her job, her career, and her reputation, Watkins was true to the truth and in a marvelous reversal of means and ends, to herself.

Good, capable individuals unconsciously guard and nurture themselves or their spirits every day in all sorts of choices, large and small. Just as their lives are never static, they are rarely if ever fractured. Their morals and ethics are never cut off from the whole of their evolving beings.

Another way to think of yourself and your life is a trajectory. Every choice you make alters that trajectory, in a positive or negative way. Will you categorize that dinner with friends as a business expense? Will you be honest with your daughter? Will you take more credit than you're due? These are just the small questions that we face every day, and little by little, the answers influence the trajectory of our lives and beings.

Another way to look at it is that life has a moral dimension. Not only is there often a right and wrong, but what goes around does come around, Karma exists, chickens *do* come home to roost, and as my mother, Phyllis, liked to say, "There is *always* a day of reckoning." The good among the great understand that every choice we make adds to the strength or weakness of our spirits—ourselves, or to use an old-fashioned word for the same idea, our souls. And that is every human's life work, to construct an identity bit by bit, to walk a path step by step, to live a life that is worthy of something higher, lighter, more fulfilling, and maybe even everlasting.

Whether you are aware of it or not, you are doing just that. Everyone is. It's inescapable. Each day constitutes another opportunity to build yourself up or tear yourself down. That is why the Reverend R. Maurice Boyd used to preach, "It's not so much that you are moral and that your enemies are immoral, but that *life itself is moral!*"[7]

Haven't you seen it? When others treat someone or some group badly, life turns on them. They're often shunned, and if dishonest, they have to compartmentalize their lives. This loss of integration in their personalities has many costs. For example, people in this state of mind can't be as expressive (chapter 17) and often have to delude themselves about their failings and standing, and that of course loosens their grip on reality (chapter 8). This trajectory puts one on a path of compromised reputation and relationships.

Personal integrity—the integration and expression of your morals and ethics in everyday life—is also derived from self-knowledge. Maslow tells us that "looking within oneself for many of the answers implies taking responsibility" for yourself.[8] Can you feel the weight? Integrity also means that the trajectory of your life starts with you. Can you imagine the possibilities? If you recognize your responsibilities, first and foremost to integrate yourself, then you can bend the arc of your future in a very positive way. And if material success is important to you, integrity is critically important. If you have it, you may just make millions or even billions as Warren Buffett and Charlie Munger have.

More Individuals Who Have Integrity: Warren Buffett and Charlie Munger

Nearly everyone with a stock portfolio knows of Berkshire Hathaway chairman and CEO, Warren Buffett. Buffett is often introduced as "the world's greatest investor." His trusted pal and vice chairman of Berkshire Hathaway is a crusty, octogenarian lawyer named Charlie Munger. Munger is less well known, though he's just as astute and entertaining as Buffett.

When I covered the Berkshire Hathaway annual meeting in 1994 for CNN, I was given just two minutes to interview Buffett and Munger. I used one of my precious questions to ask Munger if his decision "to violate his own rule to not sit on outside boards and sit on the board of directors of Costco [Wholesale Corporation] was an implicit endorsement of the stock?" He glared down at me through his extra thick glasses. (The room was so small that I had to crouch on the floor to stay out of the camera shot.) Munger was peeved not only because I was pointing out an inconsistency between his words and actions but also because I was asking him to violate his and Buffett's rule against making stock predictions. After about five agonizing seconds, Munger finally, honestly, begrudgingly spat out, "Yes." Buffett, who had turned to stare at Munger's discomfort, swung his head back to me and exclaimed with a big smile, "That's *more* than I ever get out of him!"[9]

Munger's innate honesty kept him from ducking a question that most powerful people would fudge or simply decline to answer. But fudging and ducking is not what Munger and Buffett do, especially Munger. They're fully integrated human beings so, as former U.S. senator Bill Bradley recommends, the externals of their lives truly reflect the internals. They do and say what's truly on their minds. And because they're fundamentally honest and expressive, what you see and hear is who they truly are.

They've also taken to heart Benjamin Franklin's most famous dictum: "Honesty is the best policy." They haven't done this because honesty is the nicest or the morally correct policy (though it is), but because being honest is how you build trust and value in your word. Honesty greases the wheels of social contact and by extension, business. The value of honest, ethical dealings can be summed up in one word—*reputation*. Your reputation—whether you are "reputable"—is your personal currency among everyone who knows you.

What people think of you amounts to a social store of wealth, and you're either adding to it or depleting it every day. The difference between monetary stores of wealth and social stores is that with social wealth, one failure can wipe out your entire account.

When people in Buffett or Munger's orbit ruin their reputations, they often lose Buffett and Munger as business associates and friends. At the 2009 Wesco annual meeting, Munger harkened back to his days practicing law and declared, "I would cull one client every year on moral grounds."[10]

Munger was then asked a series of questions about the roots of the financial crisis that brought down Bear Stearns and Lehman Brothers and also wounded AIG, Fannie Mae, Freddie Mac, Merrill Lynch, and so many average people. His answers all point to moral and ethical failure:

> "The salesmen who need a second pair of alligator shoes will end up cheating someone . . . a lot of discipline is needed to live a proper life."

> "The debt crisis was spawned by an irresponsible system, a lot of it, venal."

> "The scum of the earth were working in our mortgage brokerages, where some actually rejoiced at some of this flim-flam

on unsuspecting borrowers. In addition, Wall Street went crazy—where any way of making money was rationalized."

"Republican lawmakers who overdosed on Ayn Rand allowed the financial class to prey on the rest of us."

"Vendors in America should care about what they sell!"[11]

A good friend of mine asked one of Munger's daughters once what she learned from her father and she said, "The topic that I remember him harping on over and over again was honesty and character."[12]

One year later, on Friday, April 30, 2010, the eve of the Berkshire Hathaway annual meeting, Munger gave an interview to reporters Scott Patterson and Susan Pulliam of the *Wall Street Journal*. Munger, the lawyer, said he thought that the Wall Street powerhouse, Goldman Sachs, had done nothing illegal when it allegedly created and sold a security that was designed to lose value. Munger, the integrated observer of human nature, felt that the firm was engaged in "socially undesirable" activities. "They were very competitive in maximizing profits in a competitive industry that was permitted to operate like a gambling casino," he said. "The whole damn industry lost its moral moorings."[13] And that industry (investment banking) is going to be reregulated because of this loss. Echoing Boyd, Munger, at the 2009 Wesco annual meeting said, "In some sense the world is just. If you do something that is stupid, there's likely to be a whirlwind."[14]

By nearly all accounts, Buffett and Munger have been upstanding in their business dealings. Indeed, Munger argues that Buffett could have raked in billions more if he had behaved a little less ethically. "He deliberately limited his money," said Munger. "Warren would have made a lot more money if he hadn't been carrying all those shareholders."[15] Compounded over thirty-three years, the extra money would have been worth many billions—tens of billions—to him. "In the end," says Munger, "he didn't want to do it. He was competitive, but he was never just rawly competitive with no ethics. He wanted to live a certain way, and it gave him a public record and a public platform. And I would argue that Warren's life has worked out better this way."[16]

You too can live a certain way and have much more control over your destiny if you are true. You are the protagonist of your own story. Along with God, chance, or fate (whatever you call the forces you cannot control), you can also be the coauthor. While we're often buffeted by unknown and inexplicable forces, much of our destiny is ours to chart. To have better control over yours you need the support of others. Being honest, ethical and upstanding gains you that support. Just as only your own saliva can break down a stain made of your own blood, there are some things that only you can do—charting your path onto higher, more reputable, supported ground is one of them.

Be true-blue to everyone, especially yourself, and life will respond in kind.

Takeaways

Superb psychological health includes high moral and ethical behavior. And that behavior is necessary for personal growth. Life itself is moral, and honesty and ethical behavior are rewarding because they give a person authenticity, which is far more valuable than most people realize. Indeed, being authentic, according to the *Shorter Oxford English Dictionary*, makes one more "authoritative, reliable, trustworthy" and even a person "of good credit."[17]

- ✓ Karma among human beings is real. Therefore, think of life itself as moral and remember that what goes around does come around.

- ✓ Recognize that you are the product of nature, nurture, and as Dr. Stephen R. Covey says: "You are the product of choice—your choices."[18]

- ✓ Every time you are called to make a decision, remember that many choices, large and small, move you toward or away from being a better person and having a better life.

- ✓ Measure your choices by your inner, higher values more than the world's material values.

- ✓ Fight the urge to compartmentalize your choices and life. Instead, focus on creating a whole and integrated personality, routine, and existence.

Chapter 4

....

Tune Out Trends
and Traffickers

TRAIT: *UNAFFECTED*

*We only become what we are by the radical and
deep-seeded refusal of that which others have
made of us.*

—JEAN-PAUL SARTRE

ANDREW WEIL, THE ALTERNATIVE-MEDICINE pioneer we met in chapter 1, lives on a 120-acre ranch about a half-hour southeast of Tucson, where he meditates in a converted horse barn, calms his mind in a stone labyrinth, and often holds meetings in a tree house.

When interviewed by a *New York Times* reporter, Dr. Weil admitted that, yes, his home is a little "on the edge."[1] But for someone who has always gravitated to the edge of Western medicine and even the edge of U.S. culture, it suits him just fine. After all, this is the Harvard medical student who in 1964 conducted the first serious clinical studies on marijuana.

Andrew Weil's Alien Fantasy

Resisting the dominant culture, with all its subtle directives and demands, can and does make many of the best human beings feel detached from society at large, even from planet Earth. Maslow writes that "Because of this alienation from ordinary conventions and from the ordinarily accepted hypocrisies, lies, and inconsistencies of social life, they sometimes feel like spies or aliens in a foreign land and sometimes behave so."[2]

Up in Weil's wild sycamore tree house, I asked him about God and any religious feelings that he has. His answer: "I think my deepest feeling is that maybe in any life there's a feeling that something's missing, which has to do with our separation from whatever, separation from the divine or something higher."[3]

Weil went on to tell me that he believes, as many religious people believe, that he is an eternal being caught in a temporal or time-bound dimension. Moreover, just as Maslow describes, Weil sometimes feels quite un-at-home on planet Earth. He even has this recurring fantasy: "This spaceship lands and they say, 'At last, Thank God, we've found you. A horrible mistake was made! You were supposed to go to the *good* planet.'"

More than any single statement from hundreds of amazing human beings, this one made me realize that Abraham Maslow was on to something. It isn't just that the good among the great feel a real disconnect from the rest of us with our scramble to survive and our neediness. It's that people like Weil, who feel compelled to follow their own paths, are critical to self-governing democracies. According to Maslow, "Democratic self-choice society must have self-movers, self-deciders, self-choosers who make up their own minds, free agents, free-willers."[4] Here is yet another paradox—those who feel and stand apart from the rest of us are the ones who lead us.

The good among the great have a healthy degree of skepticism about current thinking and mores, advertisers and editorialists, parents and politicians, salespeople and trendsetters; in a word—they resist the zeitgeist. The good among the great don't disdain pop culture—they simply discern the paradigm in which they exist better than the average person. More than most of us, they make up their own minds and certainly don't worry about what others think of them.

There is a subtle dichotomy here—they are finely tuned perceivers of reality (see chapter 8) so they're well aware of others' reactions and opinions, but the good among the great simply don't care much about those reactions and opinions. They were the teenagers who resisted cliques and the adults who push back against the overt and covert pressures to fit in or compete. I've found that very often they grow up within families where respect for personal boundaries is high, so they are used to having and protecting their own set of convictions.

In this chapter we delve into a more subtle trait of the good among the great—an ability to ignore, even withstand group and societal pressures, to think, act, and be unaffected. This independence of thought and being makes a profound difference in one's impression of and response to the world and thus is closely linked to one's perceptions of reality and reactions to it. We learn much more about how the most successful individuals hone their perceptions of reality in chapter 8.

Maslow's Take

While the good among the great are often very distinct characters, this is not to say that the wisest among us typically stand out as eccentrics. To the casual observer, the best people appear just like everyone else, because they see little point in not going along with widely accepted codes of conduct. As Maslow puts it, "They will go through the ceremonies and rituals of convention with a good-natured shrug" rather than argue over trivialities.[5]

Though they do their best to appear to fit in, they can come across as oddballs or out-of-step. Both Abraham Lincoln and Albert Einstein were not taken seriously early in their careers because of their disheveled appearances. "When he took his chair in shabby attire with trousers too short for him, we were skeptical," recalled one eventual Einstein admirer.[6]

Because the temperamentally strong are self-sufficient (emotionally, materially, in virtually all ways), they can come across as a bit cold or aloof or even as out-of-touch eccentrics. Think of Katharine Hepburn living alone well into her nineties, carrying firewood and sailing solo off the Connecticut coast.

Though they live in harmony with their communities and cultures, the best human beings remain somewhat detached from them, just as they are a bit detached from family, and even from themselves. This trait of being so objective as to be detached is explored in much more depth in chapter 6.

Another reason that these very strong characters don't always react the way society expects them to is because their ethical standards are more finely tuned. If something isn't the way it should be, they're often the ones who stand up before anyone else. Think of Meryl Streep speaking out against pesticide residues left on factory-farmed fruits and vegetables. She did this in the 1980s—long before it was fashionable to be "organic" and way before the current "slow food" movement.

Exceptional individuals have independent minds. As Maslow puts it, they are "ruled by the laws of their own character rather than by the rules of society. It is in this sense that they are not only or merely Americans, but also, to a greater degree than others, members at large of the human species. They're not people of the decade; they're people of the century. And they're not people of a country; they're people of a planet."[7] (And maybe even people of other planets, according to Andrew Weil!) It's no wonder then that they are easily able to resist blind nationalism as well as fads, fashionistas, and sales pitches.

These are the individuals who work for international understanding and cheer on all the athletes at the Olympics instead of fixating on their country's medal count. They're like Lawrence of Arabia, who when asked by an incredulous Prince Feisal, "Are you not loyal to England?" responded, "To England, *and* to other things!"[8] Think of Tom Hanks and Clint Eastwood, two war filmmakers who have dared to portray enemy combatants in a sympathetic light. Moreover, Hanks's portrayal of an exceptionally wise dunce in *Forrest Gump* offers a brilliant portrayal of someone who has many healthy traits and a weak intellect. Forrest lives an exceptionally trying and rich life because of these virtues.

At the opposite end of the spectrum, those caught up in the zeitgeist may blindly declare, "My team—right or wrong!" They compare themselves with everyone and compete inappropriately. They worry about keeping up with the latest styles and trends. If particularly vulnerable (or gullible) they track gossip whether it's in their own circles or that of celebrities.

Even if you are not fixated on the antics of performers or pro athletes, you're still likely to be heavily influenced by the current culture. Think of style and the millions of men who now sport closely cropped facial hair, or the teenage boys with their pants falling down. Maslow writes that the vast majority of human beings "do not make up their own minds . . . They are pawns to be moved by others rather than self-moving, self-determining individuals. Therefore they are apt to feel helpless, weak, and totally determined; they are prey for predators, flabby whiners rather than self-determining, responsible persons."[9]

The good among the great easily resist society's shifting tastes and mores. Their placid demeanors, their autonomy, and their sagacity give them a kind of immunity to the common pitches, traps, and rules of national and local cultures. Their speech and manners are usually unaffected. I've found that they even speak with fewer clichés. And of course, they are far less likely to be suckered by social climbers and hucksters.

Indeed, their sensitivity and reaction to sales pitches can be strong. My friend Jim Armstrong refers to much of television as "an open sewer into your living room." What is particularly objectionable to me is that if you have a big enough budget, you can employ the cleverest salesmen and women of our age to manage our collective perceptions. Think of Chevron's "power of human energy" ads where that smooth voice is aiming to convince you of the corporation's higher ideals. And even more eerie, they often successfully sell most of us images of who *we* ought to be. These ads and thousands more like them, are invasive, pervasive, and insidious.

In their defense, corporations openly seek to influence you through paid media advertisements and public relations campaigns. Turn on any cable news channel, however, and you'll see that many of those newspeople who cloak themselves in objectivity are actually pushing their personal agendas. I covered Washington, DC for CNBC and Wall Street for CNN when objectivity was the iron rule in all newsrooms (though political objectivity is always debatable). I believed (and still believe) that a reporter's job was to be detached from the debate. Now, many anchors who have shows on news channels blatantly promote their political opinions, ideas, and ideologies. It's no surprise. In-depth, balanced, and objective news gathering is more expensive and harder work than caustic argument.

Even when playing it relatively straight, most anchors today still deliver a dramatized and combative view of events. Their language is full of war metaphors as they badger leaders, competitors, and enemies. All the while these newspeople incite us to be more or less ardent or indifferent, more or less nationalistic or cosmopolitan, more or less aggressive or passive, more or less indignant or accepting, and on and on and on. I believe strongly that one key reason the United States is at war in Iraq and Afghanistan is because the news media boost their ratings and sales by selling it. The media reflect us back to ourselves, but very often television producers and their sponsors are simply selling their programming while subtly telling us who they want us to be. When we inculcate these beguiling sales pitches, we veer off our own paths, often chasing someone else's dream or fighting someone else's fight.

How Can You Remain Unaffected?

So how do you resist all those who would lure you off of your unique path? How can you follow the example of Andrew Weil, Katharine Hepburn, Abraham Lincoln, and Albert Einstein, and become inured to the ever-present pressures to conform?

First of all, hit the switch.

There's one sure way to stem the tide of external messages: turn off the electronics. We live with a host of ways to stay "plugged in" to greater society, and the price of that connection is a constant flow of commercial, political, and social messaging. Ideally, turn off all your electronic and communication devices at a set time each day. If this proves too hard at first, start by hitting the switch once a week.

When you go on vacation, consider taking a break from television, radio, newspapers, and magazines (as well as business and commercial e-mail and texting). It's like taking a long, cleansing shower for your psyche. After you're away from the media for any extended period of time, you will be startled how silly and invasive many media messages feel.

If you live in a highly populated area, go to the beach or to hiking trails whenever possible. If you're city-bound, have picnics or go for long walks. If you can swing it, live next to a park, river, shore, or somewhere with open space near you. Best of all, live in the country! Dr. Weil has recommended for years that everyone regularly take time off from the media. He suggests taking a vacation from all news for at least one week every year.

During the rest of the year, learn to turn off the television and the radio as soon as what you're watching is over. The silence can be startling, then liberating. You'll actually be able to hear your own thoughts. Also learn to tape your favorite shows. Instead of sitting through sixteen to eighteen minutes of commercials every hour, fast-forward through them.

Dr. Stephen R. Covey, author of *The 7 Habits of Highly Effective People*, is a big proponent of turning off all electronic devices at a specific time every evening. He told me that for him, that time is seven o'clock: family dinner time. That's when he hits the switch on everything in his home—including *all* the telephones. Family dinner is a sacred time in the Covey household. This management expert reminds us not to mistake what's urgent (a ringing telephone) for what's actually important (family time). Checking your BlackBerry every fifteen minutes may seem imperative, but outside of working hours, electronic communication can be a life-sucking distraction.

What Happens in Vegas . . .

During the 1990s, Robert Higdon, who worked for the Margaret Thatcher Foundation, escorted the former prime minister of the

United Kingdom to Las Vegas. Thatcher was giving a speech about the inherent power of market economics, or some such subject. After landing, Thatcher took no notice of the sprawling strip of wild and brightly lit buildings on the way to her speech. She was busy fine-tuning her remarks.

On the way back to the airport, however, the "Iron Lady" took a moment to gaze out the window of the limousine. As she watched all the replicas fly by—the Empire State Building, the canals of Venice, and the Eiffel Tower among them—Thatcher began quizzing Higdon about what she saw, asking, in effect, "What is the Eiffel Tower doing in the middle of this desert city?"

Higdon tried to explain to her that the strip was full of renditions of famous world landmarks—that was part of the Vegas come-on.

Thatcher was incredulous. "If you're going to fly all the way to Nevada," she wondered aloud, "why wouldn't you just go to Paris or New York or Venice and see the real thing?"

"It's kind of like a fantasyland," Higdon explained. "People come here to pretend . . . and escape."[10]

"Do you mean, like an amusement park?" she asked in her proper English accent.

"Sort of," Higdon replied in his north Florida twang, "except, they're all casinos—amusement parks for adults."

Thatcher looked baffled. She just couldn't understand it. The Western leader who could see through Mikhail Gorbachev's bluster could not comprehend the average person's interest in facsimiles, when *real* versions of Venice, Paris, and New York existed.[11]

Thatcher certainly isn't stupid or imperceptive, far from it. The difference is she lives in and prefers a world of reality, not fantasy. And the draw of the crowd has no affect on her.

To people like Thatcher, a place like Las Vegas has little appeal, precisely because it's fake. The former prime minister viewed

Vegas as little more than a sales pitch, a ruse. The emphasis on gambling only proved her point. There's no better scam than casinos—which are designed to suck money out of your pocket while they sell you the hope of putting money in it. They deliver exactly the opposite of what they promise. And yet millions of people believe the hope, no matter how often it's dashed.

Healthy, happy, autonomous people don't buy the ruse. Like Thatcher, they all seem to be sticklers for what's real and authentic, not only in people but in *everything*.

Most of us hardly see the difference or even when given originals, the respect due to them because of the availability of mass-made copies. I remember being in Bellagio, Italy, and coming down a beautiful cobblestone staircase to a stunning view of sapphire-blue Lake Como, framed by snowcapped peaks. It was majestic and humbling. And then, from behind me, I heard an American woman say to her husband, "Look, Harry! It's just like the postcard!" which she then pulled from her large, colorful handbag. She and Harry proceeded to stare back and forth from the card to the view, and in the end, preferred the saturated colors of the postcard.

They had it backwards. The view wasn't gorgeous because it looked like the postcard. The postcard is a flimsy two-dimensional representation of something real and enduring.

Healthy people separate the real from the fake and never confuse the real world with the cheerful, sexualized, dramatized depictions offered by many (though not all) in the news media. They don't cringe or panic when presented by the fearful versions of the world presented by those in power who would control us.

The Costs of Accepting Others' Views

Often the costs of succumbing to zeitgeist are a lot worse than simply preferring a postcard over reality—such as the price that millions of American homeowners are now paying.

We were sold a bill of goods about the nature of home values and mortgage debt. Many of us also bought into the notion of carrying loads of consumer debt. And many highly educated government leaders took on too much public debt. When the financial system crashed in 2008, reality reared its ugly head. Americans had been sold a bill of goods about consumption; we were coaxed, wooed, and convinced to consume everything from Big Macs to "McMansions." For decades, Western marketers sold the notion that you could consume more, that you *ought* to have more, indeed, that you "deserved" more. We were endlessly convinced that you hadn't succeeded—hadn't really "arrived"—until you displayed that "more" as ostentatiously as possible.

We now have a country where two-thirds of us are overweight (one-third are obese). And as of March 2010, one-fifth of homeowners are living in houses that are worth less than the mortgages they're paying. We're a country of overeaters, choking on debt. America has become a country of salespeople feeding fat, gullible consumers. As Berkshire Hathaway vice chairman Charlie Munger constantly reminds us, salespeople are highly skilled at getting around our objections—so skilled that they can induce millions to buy what they don't need and can't afford.

As Americans, we are particularly susceptible to any kind of sales pitch that targets our national pride. The war in Iraq is a perfect example. If we can be sold a trillion-dollar war on two false premises (ties to Al Qaeda and weapons of mass destruction), we should be on guard against sales pitches that appeal to our pride or our security (or really our *in*security).

How You Can Be Unaffected

The best human beings are constantly honing their ability to sift information, discern others' motives, and judge what they perceive. This honing is an ongoing process, but it's a multifaceted habit that anyone with reasonable intelligence can develop. However, these skills require dedication and clear-sightedness.

The first thing to note about the good among the great is that, like reporters, they're natural skeptics. They question authority. Remember, they accept human nature for what it is—so they know how slipshod data is and how dastardly some people can be.

Also, high achievers are information hounds. They get good data before they make big decisions. If something doesn't add up, they get more. One expression I regularly hear from this bunch: "I don't buy it." Moreover, they're *constantly* cleaning their mental windshields.

Clean your mental windshield frequently to ensure that the messages from society, the media, and even your spouse, your parents, your friends, your colleagues, your neighbors, and whoever else seeks to influence your life are properly sifted and measured. Regularly recalibrate your moral and ethical compass to true north. You do so by developing several habits, including tuning in to those who've proved themselves to be great perceivers: your most successful friends, your wisest colleagues and associates, your happiest, most generous acquaintances. They're out there. (Those habits and much more on this are discussed in chapter 8—being realistic.)

Start today by giving yourself some distance from the world's salespeople. Turn off the car radio. Fast-forward through television ads. Consider others' motivations when they advise you. Set your sights on being more realistic, more objective, and less naïve, and seek true, independent experts when making important personal and professional choices. When I say "true," I mean that in every sense of the word. And when it comes to current culture, see it. But don't always believe it.

Takeaways

The strongest, most independent individuals actively resist current and local thinking, fashion, and salesmanship.

- ✓ Turn off all your electronic media and communication devices at a set time every evening. If this proves too difficult, commit to taking a secular sabbatical once a week.
- ✓ Take a minimum one-week holiday every year from the news.
- ✓ Record television programs, and skip the commercials.
- ✓ Recognize and resist marketers' labels and language, such as "gaming" instead of gambling, "sparkling" instead of bubbly water, and "previously owned" instead of used.
- ✓ Regularly escape societal chatter by going to parks, beaches, and the wilderness. If at all possible, live in the country!
- ✓ Don't be afraid to stand up and say, "This is wrong!" oven if no ono olco ctandc with you.
- ✓ Do what feels true to who you are—not what appears cool or fashionable to anybody else.

Chapter 5

....

Protect Your Privacy

TRAIT: *PRIVATE*

Friends will be much apart. They will respect more each other's privacy than their communion.

—HENRY DAVID THOREAU

IN EARLY 2000, THEN U.S. senator Bill Bradley from New Jersey was running for president. If anyone was going to beat Vice President Al Gore for the Democratic Party nomination, it was the lanky moderate and former basketball great. Every word Bradley uttered was splashed across most major newspapers for months, and he nearly beat Gore. Had he won, he might have gone on to beat George W. Bush.

Unlike most politicians, Bill Bradley does not particularly like being recognized. In fact, when he was a teenager and gaining notoriety around St. Louis for his skills on the basketball court, it made him a bit uncomfortable. Nevertheless, he got so good and so well known that he was offered scholarships to seventy-five colleges. He chose Princeton, where in 1964 he was named NCAA player of the year and earned a gold medal as a member of the U.S. Olympic team. Later, Bradley led the New York Knicks for ten years, winning the championship twice, and graced the cover of *Sports Illustrated* magazine.

When I asked Bradley about all the attention that he has received, starting at such a young age, he called it "well-knownness" and acknowledged that it was indeed something that he had grappled with.[1] It was one reason, he said, that he dropped out of sight after Princeton by moving to the United Kingdom on a Rhodes scholarship, and why, for a short while, he even stopped playing the game he loved.

The good among the great are not fans of fame. They recognize the superficial and false promise of it, the inherent falsehood of adulation from those who can't really know them.

Sometimes the recognition they're given even perplexes them. Liv Arnesen and Ann Bancroft are two polar explorers whom you'll hear more from in chapter 19. In the fall of 2000, when I was profiling them for the public broadcasting series *Great Leaders*, I accompanied them to New York City and the studios of ABC's *Good Morning America*. As we entered the lobby, an audience was assembled there for some other production, and the pages at the front desk announced to the crowd that Arnesen and Bancroft were "going to attempt to cross Antarctica on skis!" The crowd erupted in applause and whistles. Liv Arnesen, the cool Norwegian, turned to me and asked, "Why are they clapping?" I thought it was obvious and yelled over the uproar, "Because you're going to cross Antarctica, of course!" She looked at the beaming crowd and said, "Yes, but we haven't *done* it yet."

An irony is that the good among the great are often thrust into the public eye because of their ability, their outward focus, and their sense of obligation to help others. (We'll discuss this sense of duty in chapter 14.) But being so exposed is not often part of their agenda. When fame occurs, they pop up, take advantage of the attention to promote their goals, and then drop out of sight. Over the last three decades, business leaders have realized the value of media attention and the increased use of it.

Nonetheless, for the most part, the good among the great avoid the spotlight, for several reasons: fame exposes them and their families to envious scrutiny and criticism, the news media often make mistakes that can add up to severely distorted portrayals, family members and friends who are needy often flock to reporters to sell their personal information (the more intimate and salacious the better), and on and on. And even the most admirable people have something to hide—the inevitable strains of family relations or the lapses of youth.

But the fundamental reason that the good among the great don't get suckered into overexposure is that they simply don't *need* the recognition. These are self-assured and whole personalities. They were given or have found within themselves and their tight-knit circle of family and friends a much richer vein of positive feedback. Of course, they are human and can enjoy being idolized (witness Warren Buffett's more regular appearances these days on CNBC), but they do not *need* constant attention and have learned to be on guard against it.

With the explosion in celebrity news coverage, it's easy to pick out the troubled performers who have not learned to be on guard and who crave affirmation. Their sordid affairs, addictions, and weight problems are photographed and tracked as if they matter.

It's harder to spot the stronger souls because they elude the public gaze. Meryl Streep is one of these strong souls. The sixteen-time Academy Award nominee is, and always has been, fiercely protective of her privacy. She does not court the media and does not grant interviews unless obligated to, to promote a new movie. She does not use a social networking service and does not use her family or celebrity friends to promote herself.

When interviewed by Brad Goldfarb in the December 2002 issue of *Interview* magazine, Streep was asked why the public knows so little about her private life and the fact that she has four children. Streep responded, "Well, they're not photographed and celebrated as my appendages, no." Note Streep's reasoning is based on respect for her children's autonomy (which is discussed in depth in chapter 1). Goldfarb then asked whether protecting her privacy has been important to her work, and the actor answered with the most practical of reasons, "I don't think it helps the suspension of disbelief if everybody knows where you work out."[2]

In this chapter, we're going to talk about the fifth trait of happy, healthy, capable, and giving people: a strong desire for privacy and its correlation—solitude. This is a timely subject in an age where most of us are crowded in and around cities, and are encouraged to broadcast our most mundane and intimate experiences through Facebook, YouTube and other, free venues that can reach mass global audiences.

The good among the great guard their privacy and their time alone because they're discreet. They know that very often, personal news and information is better left unsaid. When it comes to time spent alone, they are comfortable in their own skins and actually relish mulling their own thoughts, sifting their reactions and emotions, and refining their senses of self and thus their aims, goals, and plans for the future. We'll discuss more on how the good among the great are both performance and process oriented in chapter 10. These strong individuals also recover a childlike creativity (chapter 16).

Just being alone gives you a chance to better sense your own heart and responding to that small voice inside is one of the first steps to building your unique, autonomous identity (chapter 1). A strong self-awareness is how you build independence—the kind of self-determination that propels you forward into a life that's truly yours, as well as into the larger world.

Here is where we see how each of these traits supports and flows into others. And in the trait of prizing their privacy and solitude we see how these people resuscitate themselves.

Maslow's Take

In *Motivation and Personality*, Maslow has this to say about those he dubbed "self-actualizing" people: "It's true that they can be solitary without harm to themselves and without discomfort. Furthermore, it is true for almost all that they positively *like* solitude and privacy to a definitely greater degree than the average person."[3] He goes on to write that they "are not dependent for their main satisfactions on the real world, or other people or culture or means to ends or, in general on extrinsic satisfactions."[4]

Instead, the good among the great look within themselves and to their own potential for gratification. That's why solitude is important to them. You simply can't know or develop your talents and goals if you don't actively, routinely spend time with yourself.

Albert Einstein put it this way: "I am truly a 'lone traveler' and have never belonged to my country, my home, my friends, or even my immediate family, with my whole heart; in the face of all these ties, I have never lost a sense of distance and a need for solitude."[5]

Many of us don't like being alone. We look outside ourselves for satisfaction. Sometimes we're not comfortable hearing our own thoughts, doubts, self-criticisms. Or we simply feel lonesome, even if we'll soon be with others. Being solitary without distractions opens a space and a stillness that can seem nebulous and unnerving, particularly when our sense of self isn't clearly defined and hasn't been affirmed. Crowding out that discomfort with noise, activity, and other people can be a welcome distraction. And when it comes to actual fame, these outside distractions can be seductive, even destructive.

I had a little bit of it when I was an anchor at CNN, and it is a strange beast. I would get invitations to all sorts of events only because my name was at the bottom of the small screen. I'd go to the occasional opening in Manhattan and summertime party on Long Island where I'd be introduced as "the CNN Anchorman!" This recognition fed my ego, but it also brought me unwanted scrutiny, set me apart from others, and made me one-dimensional—to many people, I was the CNN guy, and that was about it. Every introduction led to a rehash of my career, and I'd have to politely answer the inevitable questions, "How did you get on television?" "Are you ever nervous?" and "Do you write your own stories?" I bored myself and it wasn't long before I realized what thin gruel fame can be.

Nonetheless, what little recognition I had made me think twice about leaving television news. But after more than twenty years of literally chasing the high and mighty and chronicling their exploits, I wanted to cover the internal impulses and external practices of those who were not only accomplished but also good-natured. The gratification that minor-league celebrity had given me was not nearly enough to keep me in a life that I had outgrown.

For a lot of people, fame is enough. At least Roger Ailes thinks so and said as much to me in Fort Lee, New Jersey, in October of 1993. I had resigned as Washington correspondent for CNBC. I had first told Jack Welch, who was then chairman and CEO of GE, which owned NBC, which controlled CNBC. As my ultimate boss, Welch didn't want me to resign and actively tried to keep me from quitting. He got Roger Ailes, who briefly ran the business channel, to sit down at lunch with me in an effort to change my mind. After some pleasantries, Ailes asked, "So what motivates you: money, power, or fame?" I weighed each option and answered, "Well . . . I really want to produce better programming . . . and . . . I would like more responsibility in that direction."

"Yeah, yeah," he muttered in between bites from an enormous platter of spaghetti and meatballs. "But really, which is it—money, power, or fame?"

He lost me right there. Two weeks later I left CNBC to handle corporate communications for Barry Diller at QVC. Don't get me wrong. Money, power, and fame are alluring—particularly money and power. But there's a lot more that motivates me and many other people, particularly the good among the great. Not only are those of us who have a true, whole sense of self interested in doing quality work, we want to have a positive impact.

What I didn't realize is that many people aren't even aware of their deeper, quieter motivations and thus they don't know how valuable they are and what a counterweight they can be to money, power, and fame. A dozen years later, after also reporting and anchoring business news for CNN, I came back to New York for a social visit. At one event in Southampton, a correspondent I knew from ABC Television's *20/20* came up to me at a party and said, "How did you do it? You just walked away!" He was tipsy and confessed that he was exhausted by all the travel and pressure of his job, the endless disaster chase, and lack of a private life. And yet he couldn't quit. He was psychologically trapped, unable to leave the recognition and status of being on television. I was able to walk away from the minor league glamour of CNBC and CNN and it flabbergasted him.

In the best-selling business book *Good to Great*, Jim Collins writes about what he calls Level 5 Leaders: men and women who carry "no airs of self-importance." Collins describes them as compellingly modest, with "quiet, dogged natures."[6] Many of these humble high-achievers sacrifice their solitude and private lives so that they may help the greater good: build companies, lead organizations, and push new technologies and better ways of doing business. They very often turn up in the public realm to do some significant job, and then, when they're done, disappear without a word. Most exemplary human beings don't hang on to the microphone, craving the spotlight. In fact, they don't crave much of anything. They would happily live their lives without being observed and letting that observation distort them.

Indeed, I have three longstanding family friends who've made hundreds of millions if not billions of dollars through venture capital or private equity investing. Much to my frustration, all three have repeatedly declined to do personal interviews with me or anyone else. As one explained years ago when he was cornered by a business magazine writer, "A whale is harpooned only when it spouts."

Virtually all great and good individuals exhibit this preference for privacy and regular time alone. The more recognition they face, the more strongly they feel the need to protect their private lives, their families, and their alone time. One reason that they are more protective is because they're more genuine than most of us. It's unnatural for them to craft a persona—for public consumption or any other reason. Their natural spontaneity, expressiveness, and honesty can betray them. Thus, the spotlight of media attention can be particularly revealing for these genuine individuals.

No matter how many cameras she's faced, Meryl Streep still "hates" being photographed.[7] Portrait photographer Brigitte Lacombe, who's taken Streep's picture on dozens of occasions, says, "With Meryl, it's a complete struggle to get her to stay in front of the camera."[8] One reason is humility. For the modest, it's uncomfortable to be celebrated. But it may also be that she can't help but reveal much of herself, too much for a private person. Those who are true, whole persons are more sincere and their countenances more true, so the rest of us can see into them. It's a marvel and very attractive. Though for people like Streep, it's invasive.

Even if you're never thrust into the public forum or cheated of your alone time, let these talented individuals inspire you to celebrate your solitude and prize your private life.

Takeaways

Privacy is precious, fame is worth little, and solitude is an opportunity for self-discovery and emotional resuscitation.

- ✓ Prize and protect your privacy with vigilance. Remember, "A whale is harpooned only when it spouts."
- ✓ Spend at least several hours each week in your own company, without the distractions of television, the Internet, or other people.
- ✓ If you're seeking satisfaction through recognition, you are not seeking it from within—from your own potentialities.
- ✓ If recognized, remember the cycle of human commentary—If you're celebrated today, you'll be torn down tomorrow.
- ✓ Use the solitary moments in your life to seek intense calm and quiet so that you may sense your deepest wants, needs, emotions, and reactions. Use this time to refine your goals and plan your strategies to achieve them.
- ✓ Remember that fame is a barrier to true communication with most other people.

Chapter 6

···

Stand Back!

TRAIT: *DETACHED*

*You must be willing to meet existential
suffering and work it through.*

—M. SCOTT PECK

MARY CUNNINGHAM[1] IS THE most remarkable
woman you've never heard of. Of the hundreds of amazing people
I've interviewed over the years, this seventy-five-year-old grandmother of six remains one of the best examples of a self-actualizing person I've ever met.

I've known Mary since I was five or six years old. My family
was lucky enough to spend some time each summer on a beautiful lake in Ontario, Canada. There, the Cunningham household
was my second home, a refuge from my parents' divorce and my
own concerns. The Cunninghams returned every summer to a
beautiful old family house, green and white with sleeping porches

and a children's nursery filled with pint-sized furniture. That gracious old home was where I spent a lot of my time and where I learned how to be happy. The Cunningham children were like siblings to me. Jimmy was my best friend; Cathy and Melinda were like sisters. And Mary, their mom, was my "other mother." My own mom called Mary "The Countess" not only because that was the name of the old wooden boat she drove but also because she was, and is, noble in character.

Mary always exhibited an intriguing mix of common sense and dignity. For me and all the children we knew on the lake, she was welcoming and supportive without being intrusive. The Cunningham household was simply the best atmosphere around, which explains why so many kids gathered and continue to gather there. It was laid back and fun. The Cunninghams are athletic and always open to new experiences so there were always new games and toys, such as a trampoline and wake boards. There was always great food, fun, houseguests, and more. The Cunninghams even invented their own poker game, which we would play for hours on rainy days, interrupted only by batches of hot cookies.

This is also a family that seemed to find humor everywhere: in word puns, the absurdity of kids' antics, limericks, old jokes, and musty old costumes dragged from a tin-lined storage room. I vividly remember laughing nonstop for hours the first day that Jimmy arrived the summer I was eleven years old.

As I've grown older, I've come to recognize and appreciate the traits that make the Cunninghams such a happy clan and their matriarch, Mary, such an extraordinary human being. Foremost among these is Mary's objectivity, her ability to stand back from herself and her environment in ways that most of us simply do not, or cannot, do. Mary is a stoic in many ways, coolly accepting life for what it is without drama or complaint. It isn't that she represses her emotions. Instead, she has an acceptance of life for what it is, as well as an acceptance of others that was profoundly reassuring to me as a boy.

I talked at length with Mary's daughters, Cathy and Melinda, about their mom in February of 2010. When I asked if Mary was affectionate as a mom, both Cathy and Melinda replied, "No, not at all. She never said 'I love you' to us. However, we never doubted her love . . . Never, never, never did we doubt it."[2] Both daughters say that they are more demonstrative with their own children and ascribe Mary's reticence as "part of that generation and a WASP thing."[3] Maybe, but from my standpoint her behavior is more a reflection of Mary's overall personality. She has a dramaless detachment that may seem foreign to most of us, and yet, it's one of the traits Maslow identified over and over in the highly evolved personalities he admired, and a trait I've witnessed in the good among the great whom I've profiled.

Mary's detachment made her aware of and respect personal boundaries, even those of young children. According to Cathy, "She gave us huge independence. Dad was detached too. They did not get overly involved. She was nurturing but also gave us huge independence, which I think made us more secure in ourselves . . . My mom was not always at the back door waiting for me when I got home from school."

Melinda added, "I crawled through the milk chute a number of times to get into that house because Mom would be late from a tennis date."[4]

In a culture where helicopter parenting is more the norm, this kind of parenting may seem inattentive, but Mary's looser, more respectful parenting style is one reason her own kids consider her a great mom. She didn't smother them. She didn't project her needs, wants, and worries on them. She loved them while also allowing them the space they needed to grow into self-confident, resourceful individuals.

Her objective outlook showed up in other ways as well. Like Poosie and Charlie Orr, Mary was not a strict disciplinarian. She demonstrated rather than imposed discipline. Thus, her home, appearance, finances, and schedule were all carefully and thoughtfully organized. She cooked marvelous and creative meals every day, played tennis every Friday, held investment club meetings once a month, and planned constantly: new plays and concerts as well as adventurous family travel. Throughout, Mary was cheerfully even-tempered. "When I was a teenager, I found her to be so in control of her emotions," Cathy admitted, "so calm, so controlled, that at times it blew my mind."[5]

Neither Cathy nor Melinda struggled with their mother during their teenage years—unusual among adolescent girls. Today they recognize that this is because Mary let them lead relatively independent lives. "She respected us," said Melinda. Now both Cathy and Melinda have daughters of their own, and the remarkable tradition continues: there are no struggles for freedom, no nasty fights over boys, booze, or studies. They respect their daughters' wants and needs and have joyfully nurtured *their* growth and independence.

According to Cathy, Mary was and is "unflappable. Just like a duck—lets water roll right off her back." To use Maslow's phrasing, she "remains unruffled," someone who doesn't get flummoxed by the frustrations of daily existence or the deep disappointments we all suffer in life. As far as a philosophy of life, she doesn't appear to have one, let alone worry about having one. Cathy puts it succinctly—for her mom, she says "Life isn't something that you need to go searching for. It's right there in front of you."[6]

That's the fundamental wisdom that the Buddha discovered after a youth of princely indulgence and then six agonizing years of self-denial and reflection. Mary Cunningham—a housewife and mom from Pittsburgh—lives this wisdom, without ever studying a word of Buddhism or uttering a single "Om."

Detachment Tested

Mary's detachment has been tested in three profound ways. One came in late 1993, when Melinda was diagnosed with full-blown AIDS. You'll read more on that in chapter 9.

Test number two for Mary's stoic detachment: Parkinson's disease. Mary is now in the advanced stages of Parkinson's. This graceful, collected, articulate woman is now a shaking bundle of missteps and forgotten words. It's a cruel, progressive malady and one that Mary has not complained about, not once. According to Cathy, "She has never asked, 'Why me?'"[7]

But by far the most difficult challenge to Mary Cunningham's calm detachment happened some thirty years ago, when she was in her midforties. One day, a burglar followed the Cunninghams' housekeeper to their house, followed her in, tied her up, stole some jewelry, and finding Mary, raped her at gunpoint.

Rape would shake most people to the core. Even the word rattles some of us. Many victims of sexual violence never fully recover. And yet, Mary emerged from the rape seemingly un-scathed. She did not and has not let it touch her being. Cathy says that her mom has hardly mentioned it to her, and Melinda says her mom has never spoken about it to her. In fact, the day that it happened, Mary served her family a homemade dinner—which still flabbergasts her daughters.

Moreover, not long after the incident occurred, the rapist was captured and Mary faced him down with her testimony in court. He served three years in prison. What impact the whole terrifying episode had on this remarkable woman we do not know because she does not show it. We do know that she has never made her children feel worried or scared for her.

People may find it easy to accuse Mary Cunningham of being in denial, but not once have I witnessed any repercussions from the rape. Nor has anyone in the family ever described any residual issues. I once asked Mary about it, and she simply shook her head and muttered, "*Bad!*" Enough said.[8]

I believe it is because of her extraordinary objectivity, detachment, and even self-transcendence that Mary Cunningham could withstand such brutality with such reserve. Some people might find her reaction shocking, baffling, or just strange, but I find it fitting for her and a sign of great personal strength.

The good among the great are like Mary. When you first meet them, they can come across as a little bit cool, or aloof. They don't gush or demand attention. They're a bit reserved about their assessments and opinions. Their judgments are thought through and always their own. Wisely, they tend to let others speak first. And they're always objective. They simply don't have a lot of emotional baggage that makes their thinking subjective. They don't turn a conversation around and make it about them. They're like good mediators in that they have some distance from their thoughts and their selves. Strong psyches remain unruffled by the events that rattle the average person. This ability to remain centered makes the good among the great resilient. Detachment is a key reason that they are resilient. In truth, they simply don't suffer emotionally from setbacks the way the rest of us do.

They are not superhuman, and in moments of extreme stress, they also can panic. But their reactions to danger, extreme excitement, and terrible news are muted, if not explicitly controlled. Steve Case of AOL told me that he felt a bit like a shock absorber—being purposely upbeat to encourage employees when, early in AOL's history, there were a few well-publicized service failures. Alternately, he tamped down expectations and excitement when AOL was racking up huge subscriber gains.

To quash her own panic when she fell into a crevasse while hiking in Antarctica, Liv Arnesen, the Norwegian polar explorer whom we first met in chapter 5, forced herself to recollect a prior summer's vacation, right down to the games she played with her children.

Whether they are born with exceptionally calm demeanors or they learn to have some distance from their emotions, the good among the great I've profiled develop a true, whole sense of themselves and are both aware of and a bit detached from their feelings and reactions.

Maslow's Take

In his analysis of self-actualizing individuals, Abraham Maslow described people who are so independent from their environments that they stay calm "in the face of hard knocks, blows, deprivations, frustrations, and the like."[9]

In *Motivation and Personality*, he describes the apparent paradox of detached but loving people. These people he writes, "maintain a degree of individuality, detachment, and autonomy that seems at first glance to be incompatible with the kind of identification and love that I have been describing."[10] Take Mary Cunningham as an example—she is very loving to her family and many, many others, though she doesn't express it in an overt or demonstrative way. She can even come across as a bit cool.

"But this is only an apparent paradox," Maslow continues. "As we have seen, the tendencies to detachment and to profound inter-relationships with another person *can* coexist in healthy people. The fact is that self-actualizing people are simultaneously the most individualistic and the most altruistic and social and loving of all human beings."[11]

Maslow argues that our culture has made a mistake by putting these qualities at opposite ends of a single continuum. We assume that detached and objective people cannot be warm, loving people at the same time, but in reality, they can. "These qualities go together," Maslow explains, "and that dichotomy is resolved in self-actualizing people."[12]

Mary Cunningham's ability to maintain her inner sense of calm despite her daughter's AIDS diagnosis, her own Parkinson's disease, and her experience of rape demonstrates an ability to consciously disassociate herself—in a healthy way—from a traumatic experience. Those who meditate are able to experience a sense of "being outside" or "witnessing" themselves at times of great stress or excitement. However it's analyzed, Mary Cunningham's cool reserve allowed her to withstand the assault psychologically.

Maslow's thoughts: "It is often possible for them to remain above the battle . . . to remain unruffled, undisturbed by that which produces turmoil in others. They find it easy to be aloof, reserved, and also calm and cool. It becomes possible for them to take personal misfortunes without reacting violently as the ordinary person does."[13] Mary's husband, Robert, wanted with all his heart to react violently against his wife's assailant. Mary would have none of it, and without much more than a shrug, accepted her misfortune and put it behind her.

This control, or more accurately, this detachment from emotions, is a critical necessity for mastery of many Eastern martial arts. It's also a state of mind that religious people seek as they confront all the violence and cruelty of the world. It is the elevated state of calm that can imbue people with extraordinary skill. It's often described in literature and portrayed in film, even mass market movies, such as *Star Wars*. In *Return of the Jedi,* the plot reaches its emotional crescendo when the emperor attempts to turn Luke Skywalker to the "dark side," saying, "Give in to your anger . . . with each passing moment you make yourself more my servant . . . I feel your anger. Strike me down with all of your hatred, and your journey toward the dark side will be complete!"[14] Skywalker briefly gives in to his anger and strikes at the Dark Lord of the Sith. Darth Vader blocks the blow and a fierce light-saber duel ensues. Skywalker eventually wins that struggle, but only after regaining the calm and philosophical detachment that flows from the "Force."

Other Benefits and By-products of Detachment

Several perks (besides slaying evil emperors) result from developing this sort of objective detachment. Resilience in facing hard knocks as well as extraordinary calm during a crisis are two. An unusual ability to concentrate is a third. "We have seen that they are more problem-centered than ego-centered," Maslow says. "This is true even when the problem concerns themselves—their own wishes, motives, hopes, or aspirations. Consequently, they have the ability to concentrate to a degree not usual for ordinary people."[15] Sometimes this concentration produces by-products like absent-mindedness and obliviousness to dress codes and surroundings. These by-products are reasons these individuals can come across as aloof or eccentric. But this obliviousness is only because mundane activities are secondary to the problem being tackled.

How Can You Become More Detached?

Suspending the analytical mind by practicing simple meditation is a free and flexible way to condition yourself to be more detached. Meditating doesn't need to be an elaborate exercise—you can do it in ninety seconds by simply staying still, focusing on your breathing, slowly reconnecting with all your senses, and gently clearing your mind of thought. With a little practice, you can learn to do it virtually anywhere. The toughest part is to gently quiet the continuous chatter of our caffeinated minds. But if you are persistent and again, gentle about it, you will succeed. Reconnecting with your senses—particularly your hearing—will help you be more outwardly focused and obviously, a better listener.

Meditating allows you to get some separateness from your own thoughts, and thereby helps you develop the calm objectivity of a Mary Cunningham or a Jedi Knight. There are other ways: a good, long walk in nature will also help you get some distance from current thinking as well as your own. Aerobic exercise does it as well. I have no doubt that all those long distance cyclists, runners, and swimmers are enjoying these benefits, whether they realize it or not.

There are a number of other ways to distract ourselves from our own nagging and niggling minds. Engaging in hobbies, particularly those that require use of our hands, as well as listening to music, are classic ways that we relax. Working and playing with animals are two more ways to turn your focus outward.

Our reasoning mind is a marvel of evolution—the most developed part of the human brain, and it's how we build and manage our modern civilizations. But for high achievers—it's in hyperdrive every day. Shutting it off and reconnecting with our physical, sensory, creative, and spiritual selves refreshes our whole being and allows us to tap into a deeper, older wisdom.

Even though wise men and women have practiced separating themselves from their thoughts for eons, for many of us today, it feels like a foreign concept. It seems Eastern or worse, New Age. In school, we're not taught to doubt what we think. We think therefore we are, right? And yet so much current research finds that our thinking is often flawed. So how do we better judge our own thinking? According to Maslow and virtually every good soul among the high achievers I've met, the answer is more objectivity, more detachment, and if you are lucky, even self-transcendence.

Integrated medicine pioneer Andrew Weil also argues that we should have some detachment from our own thinking. This is what the wise doctor told me about the practical benefits of stillness, deep breathing, and clearing your mind of thoughts: "On a very mundane level, it's a good relaxation method. It's also a way to restructure the mind . . . a way to have some spaciousness or freedom about always paying attention to your thoughts. Meditation trains you to be less reactive in the rest of your day. That is, to be more grounded, more centered in the calm place inside yourself which makes you more effective dealing with the world."[16]

Notice that Weil is not talking about transcendental experience or love or global peace. He's talking about control over the way you react, as well as greater effectiveness.

Being effective means having the power to achieve your purposes. Weil argues that getting more separation from your thoughts, being calmer, more centered and thus focused on your goals, makes you more powerful.

In the same way, best-selling author Stephen R. Covey believes that making better choices, large and small, requires "widening the space between what happens to you in your life and how you react to it." You can learn to get some distance from your thoughts, emotions, and reactions through prayer, meditation, and even just deep breathing and counting to ten before you react. If you do, according to Covey, you widen the space between what happens to you and how you react. You can achieve a calmer and more objective view of life, others, and yourself.[17] This is critical in terms of giving yourself a shot at better life choices. You may even grasp greater wisdom, and a lasting sense of calm.[18]

You just might, as Mary's daughter Cathy said, "Get the joke about life . . . Don't get me wrong, life isn't a joke, but it's not something that you need to go searching for . . . *it's right there in front of you.*"[19]

Takeaways

Objectivity leads to more calm and more reasoned responses to the world. Deep objectivity gives you a level of detachment, even from calamity. This stoicism can make you more resilient, more respectful and stronger temperamentally. A measure of detachment is a very valuable state of being—one that supports serenity, focus, and achievement.

- ✓ Quiet your internal mind chatter with meditation, nature, creative pursuits, music, and exercise.
- ✓ When assessing important situations and jobs clear your mind first. Use deep breathing while you reconnect with your five senses. Afterward your analytical mind will be less subjective and more focused on the situation at hand.
- ✓ When making group judgments and decisions let others make their comments before offering your assessment.
- ✓ Don't be afraid of appearing detached, odd, or aloof; intense concentration may make you appear this way to others.
- ✓ Reject the notion that detached people are not loving. It is our culture that has erected a false dichotomy between the two.
- ✓ If you're a parent, don't smother your children. Respect them enough to honor their independence. That's respectful, not needy love.
- ✓ Demonstrate rather than impose discipline.

Part 2

Assessing the World Clearly and Efficiently

Chapter 7

···

Get Out the Door

TRAIT: *EXPERIENTIAL*

I don't need faith. I have experience.

—JOSEPH CAMPBELL

IN HIS LATE TWENTIES, Barry Diller, the media and technology tycoon, made the ABC television network number one in ratings. In the 1980s he helped build Paramount Studios. Then under Rupert Murdoch, he cobbled together the Fox television network. In the 1990s he bought into and ran QVC, the home shopping channel, before building Interactive Corporation—a host of on-line consumer companies. This is a restless mogul who is many things. Among them, he's experiential.

Like most entrepreneurial leaders, Barry loves change: anticipating it, calculating it, debating it, and most of all, initiating and prospering from it. I once watched him select bites of food from four dinners at once, moving around a small table and sampling the different dishes he'd ordered sent up to his apartment at the Waldorf Astoria. A colleague once described this mercurial man as being "just like a kid" at a lavish Hollywood party where carnival rides were set up. Barry had rushed from the Ferris wheel to the bumper cars, indeed to all the rides, just like a child.

I handled communications for Barry for nearly a year when he was running QVC. I would not describe Barry Diller as self-actualizing. He was fearsome, short-tempered, and showed virtually no empathy for those who worked for him. But he was, and forced those around him to be, open to experience. He wanted proof first-hand of any proposal you made. And he loved to shake us up so that we were scrambling to improve the quality and speed of our data gathering, our communications, and our customer service. He would insist on tearing up whole systems on a regular basis just to improve our performance a little bit. Barry's forward momentum kept us all on our toes.

His appetite for new experiences and conquests had and continues to have him hunting for the next big opportunity, the next technology, even the next industry. During my tenure with him at QVC, we tried to take over Paramount Communications. Ultimately we were outbid, despite putting a $10 billion offer on the table. In late December of 1993, Sumner Redstone's Viacom outbid us with a complicated package of cash and securities that amounted to some $10.6 billion. In defeat, Barry gave me a five word statement to issue to the world, "They won. We lost. Next." That evening, two of the three television network news anchors quoted Barry and not Redstone. Barry snatched a PR win out from under a $10 billion loss. And he did it by focusing on the future—his next big experience.

Around 11:00 p.m. that night I delivered the first edition of the *New York Times* and the *Wall Street Journal* up to Barry and his then girlfriend and now wife, Diane Von Furstenberg. Barry was calm and matter-of-fact, not unhappy at all. Even Diane seemed a little surprised by his stoic stance. I suspect that Barry was already contemplating his next target, which, six months later, turned out to be CBS.

I've found that like Barry, the highest achievers thrive on steep learning curves and get rapidly bored with the status quo. Sabeer Bahtia, the cofounder of Hotmail, told me in September of 2000 that creative and ambitious people are always looking for their next job within two years of landing their current positions.[1] I didn't believe him until he quizzed me about my career, and I had to admit that I had always begun plotting my next move within two years of landing any given job. Often I wanted to stay within the company, even the division where I was, but I always wanted a different, more creative, or more responsible position.[2]

Human resources executives take note! The good among the great want new experiences. They like a challenge, being a bit off balance, and having to stretch, because for them, adrenaline is not only exciting, it heightens their awareness. For most people, mastering a job is the goal because it's more comfortable. For the restless, mastery is also the goal, but once achieved, it is *un*comfortable. They don't just accept constant change—they welcome it, even play with it. And this goes for everything, not just work. They want to stimulate their senses as well as their imaginations. They are, to use Maslow's language, more open to experience. And it is precisely this openness that opens doors for many of the great joys and successes in their lives.

In this chapter, we'll look at how being experiential manifests itself in, and contributes to, the lives of happy, healthy, capable individuals. We'll discuss how being open to experience is critical to finding your path because experimenting with what you do, how you live, and what you believe aides you in finding out who you are and where you're headed. Only if you know where you belong, with whom you want to be, and what you want to do will you know who you truly are and how you can best contribute to others and to the world.

Maslow's Take

Abraham Maslow described self-actualizing people as having "more openness to experience." Happy high achievers aren't just interested or inquisitive—though they are. They just take it further. They like to try things on. It's a holistic way of learning. This trait of openness means going beyond textbook learning to embody an active, adventurous experimentation. In slang terms, the good among the great are "game," or as Australians put it, they like to "give it a go!"

To act is to prepare, attempt, exert, feel the exhilaration and exhaustion, and witness the repercussions of what you're feeling, thinking, and doing. You get to test your theories and assumptions, so you're brought closer to reality. Acting also gets you closer to yourself—your likes, dislikes, fears, and wonders. It can also bring you closer to others. Jump off a thirty-foot cliff into a lake with friends, and you have shared something visceral.

To act means getting off the tour bus of life (for example watching television) and living among the locals, allowing worlds other than your own to stimulate your senses. It means smelling, tasting, sensing, and feeling as others feel. As Warren Buffett once put it, "Can you really explain to a fish what it's like to walk on land? One day on land is worth a thousand years of talking about it."[3]

Be Open to Others' Experience

Being truly open to experience means going beyond sensory experimentation; it involves existential questioning. If the strongest among us know who they are, what they believe, and where they want to go, one reason they know all that is because they are constantly testing and refining their knowledge by experiencing alternative ways of being, thinking, and behaving. Healthy individuals want to feel as others feel. They're empathic to others. (We'll discuss this further in chapter 13.) So, very often they want to experience what others experience. They dive into other cultures, delve into other ethics, and study other gods. They want to hear and speak the languages (is there any sexier word than "amour" pronounced properly?), enter the buildings, smell the air, wear the clothes, taste the cooking, and most of all, be with those who are different. So many of the friends I admire not only travel extensively but live in other countries for a while. As young people, they do it on shoestring budgets and when they get older, they rent out-of-the-way houses and apartments. They sink into the foreign culture and discover more about humanity and themselves.

The best human beings enjoy subsuming themselves amidst what's new, exotic, and even strange. This is a kind of egalitarian humility. In chapter 11 we'll learn how the best beings are explicitly nonhierarchical. They give virtually everyone a measure of real respect, and as Maslow puts it, "they find it possible to learn from anybody who has something to teach them—no matter what other characteristics he or she may have."[4] This is why billionaires sit in rapt attention to children and society matrons fawn over native Canadian moccasin makers. In these situations, the best people don't exert any hierarchical standing. The reason is that they know how little they know.

The good among the great are calm when facing the unknown (chapter 9) so they don't halt themselves, fearful of what may happen to them if they try something new. It's not that they're reckless. The great and good people I've known are not just out for thrills. They're curious about how others live and willingly experiment with their own routines. They don't mind taking minor risks in their lives because they're realists (chapter 8). They are typically very good at assessing and minimizing downside risk.

They're also preparers who carefully plan their excursions into exotic places and ideas. They have no desire to remain mired in old habits or routines. That would be static and dissatisfying. It would fly in the face of reality since the world is constantly changing.

Because *everything is always evolving*, you need to constantly update your perceptions of the world, and there's no better way to do that than through immersion. My most compelling experience in immersion was with language as a first and second grader. I attended the Toronto French School, where all the courses as well as recess, lunchtime, and sports activities were conducted not only in French but also as if we were French. I studied the history and geography of France. We read French stories and sang French songs. After a few months, I not only spoke better French than English, I thought and dreamt as a Parisian boy would. There is no way you can fully comprehend the French, or any foreign mentality, until you mouth their words and dream their dreams.

So, being experiential is not only stimulating, it is a lifelong education and reality check. The strongest, happiest people are actually eager to test, measure, and even challenge their own thinking and behavior by trying new thinking and behavior on for size.

People who are open to experience are also infinitely more adaptable because their minds continue to grow to fit each new environment they explore. Sometimes that requires drumming up courage or a willingness to test your belief systems, broaden your sense of beauty, or hone your perception of what is lasting and true. And to take it one step further, it means swimming deeply in who you are and who you aim to be.

As Bill Bradley, the former U.S. senator from New Jersey, told me, "Feeling is as important as thinking."[5] Bradley would know since he spent the first half of his life "feeling" as well as working his way to dominance on the basketball court. In current market-based societies, thinking is what is rewarded. Tasking the analytical part of our brains in finely specialized fields (finance, law, engineering, management, etc.) is how we boost our salaries and push ahead of rivals.

But Bradley, who is wiser and more philosophical than most politicians or athletes, argues that your sensory and emotional responses are just as valuable as your deepest reasoning when it comes to guiding your life. The point is that it is one thing to watch someone get a three-pointer in a basketball game or be interviewed on live television or ski a black diamond slope, but it's quite another to experience those activities yourself.

If you're unconvinced, then invert the question. Are those who avoid new experiences more likely to be more aware, more astute and discerning individuals? The answer is obvious. We all know people who actively avoid new experiences. For example, I know a guy who lives less than three miles from his parents' house. For thirty-five years he's had just two jobs, performing virtually the same tasks among many of the same people. He takes the same vacations every year and watches the same television shows every week. He even sits in the very same chair every time he's at home! His mind-set is frozen, his prospects stagnant as a result. His story is a life of experiences missed.

More People Who Are Experiential

The Cunningham family you met in chapter 6 are the opposite in outlook and action. They were and are always trying new things. Until slowed with Parkinson's, Mary, the matriarch, was always organizing new adventures for the whole family—bicycling trips, concerts, whitewater rafting, plays, kayaking, even parasailing. The Cunninghams have skied every great slope in the

West, cavorted with wildlife in the Galapagos Islands, read most of the books on the bestseller lists, and tried every new board game. Meanwhile, my family gathered year after year at the same sunny watering holes and drank. When it rained, we watched television.

An outward focus and experiential nature propels the Cunninghams to take trips to new destinations, cook and devour all kinds of recipes, and meet new people. But, as the late, great professor of comparative religion, Joseph Campbell, pointed out, being open to experience also means being *inwardly* curious. That means trying new ways of "being" and challenging the status quo within yourself. This has to be why virtually all my old pals on the lake in Canada relish a good costume party. It gives them a few days to literally fabricate and don a new persona. My favorite getup so far was being "Fat Bastard" from the *Austin Powers* movies. Despite the kilt, it was surprisingly warm and comforting to be enveloped in foam rubber blubber.

Great achievers have a firm sense of identity and strongly held convictions, yet oftentimes, it's this desire to push themselves out of their comfort zones that confirms and refines those convictions. Therefore, they have a more nuanced and sophisticated sense of who they are and who they're becoming. They often know exactly what they stand for because they've been trying on new ideas and challenging their own arguments. They test and measure their own ideas, beliefs, and capabilities against a constantly changing set of backdrops, companions, and competitors.

On the PBS series *The Power of Myth*, Joseph Campbell told Bill Moyers that we are not seeking the meaning of life as much as "the experience of being alive, so our life experiences on the physical plane will have resonances within our innermost reality and being—so we'll feel the rapture of being alive!"[6]

Rapture? When was the last time you even used the word? According to the *Shorter Oxford English Dictionary*, rapture has several meanings, though for our purposes, it means "a state of passionate excitement."[7] Everyone wants rapture. Unfortunately, rapture rarely comes to us sitting on our sofas. Deep-sea divers sink deep below the surface of the water to experience a version of this feeling. Religious people chant and pray to achieve it. Athletes and performers work for decades to "be in the zone." (You'll find more on this in chapter 19.) The point is you have to *do* something to achieve passionate excitement.

Takeaways

You have to *act* to truly know. As the nineteenth-century American philosopher William James put it, "To begin anything, it is not word or thought or power that matters; it is the act that matters."[8]

- ✓ Try a new route to work. Better yet, try walking or riding a motorcycle to work.
- ✓ Take your next vacation in a place you've never been. Use vacations to discover vocations.
- ✓ Choose one night a week to cook and taste new foods or go to a restaurant in a part of town where you don't typically venture.
- ✓ Read a book in a genre you've never read.
- ✓ Wear a piece of clothing that is distinctly foreign.
- ✓ Hand out silly hats and masks at your next party.
- ✓ Take a class in some subject you've always found intriguing.
- ✓ If religious, pray in a place of worship that is unfamiliar, even foreign to you.
- ✓ If you've never dressed in drag, you're overdue!

Chapter 8

....

Don't Kid Yourself!

TRAIT: *REALISTIC*

Mental health is an ongoing process or
dedication to reality at all costs.

—M. SCOTT PECK

ONE LEADING ENTREPRENEUR WHO used his supe-
rior perception of reality to build the on-line powerhouse AOL
is Steve Case. His now-deceased brother Dan, a business success
in his own right as head of San Francisco–based investment bank
Chase H&Q, told me in 2000 that even as a boy, Steve was always
able to "participate and watch . . . Steve was always really good at
participating and watching and perhaps that's why this interactive
medium, though in its earlier stages was less personal, he so in-
nately understood."[1]

In other words, Steve Case was always watching, listening, even when he himself was actively involved. That's like being the coach while also playing on the team.

At AOL, Case's nickname was "the Wall" because in nearly any kind of meeting or interview, he would sit blank-faced. This was the watcher in him. He was supposed to be participating and he was, in his own way. But he would give very little feedback. His poker face was unnerving to those who worked with him. According to Case himself, he only appears this way because his senses are wide open, receptive, as he looks and listens for clues to what's going on, to people's motivations, to what they're *not* saying, to group dynamics, to shifting assessments, to bits of market data that no one else notices, to who's really prepared, and on and on.

Case is exquisitely sensitive to information—absorbing it, sorting it, filing and re-organizing it. This is how he put it to me in an interview from 2001: "It's just sort of being able to soak things up . . . it's sort of like a pattern recognition kind of experiment . . . hearing this, reading this, seeing that, thinking that, being able to connect the dots in your head even when they're not so easily connectable. That is like having a pulse to what's happening."[2]

In the early 1980s, that pulse gave Case his "genius moment," according to *Aol.com* author and *Wall Street Journal* contributor Kara Swisher—the revelation that the computer could and would be about mass communication and virtual communities, not just a tool for engineers and a toy for geeks. Steve Case's relentless data gathering and sorting skills helped him divine the future.[3]

It certainly helped him see opportunity in structuring the $164 billion merger of AOL with Time Warner in January 2000 just before the dot-com bubble burst. The merger ended up being a failure—mainly for Time Warner shareholders. But Case made a fortune by, in effect, selling AOL at the top of the market.

And he's had other hits, including a company called Revolution Money, which was bought by American Express in November 2009 for $300 million.

Maslow's Take

Abraham Maslow wrote that the best among us have a "greater freshness, penetration, and efficiency of perception."[4] He argues that their sense of what's going on is less skewed by their own emotional baggage (freshness) and they have a kind of x-ray vision into people as well as situations (penetration). He also wrote that these individuals—whom he dubbed "self-actualizing"—"get it" about everything with less effort than the rest of us (efficiency). Imagine the advantages in business strategy, choosing investments, finding a spouse, everything!

First and foremost, healthy human beings are realistic about themselves. Most of us don't critically examine our "selves"—our strengths and weaknesses, faults and foibles, fears and longings. As we learned in chapter 1, knowing yourself is the first step to achieving your goals. We don't often test our assumptions and look at the repercussions of our actions. The good among the great are well aware of their shortcomings because they continuously assess them and work to compensate or overcome them. They also find partners, personal and professional, who complement their strengths and compensate for their weaknesses.

It's important to note that Maslow is talking specifically about "perception." Being a discerning and objective perceiver of the world and one's self may be a trait some are born with, but just about anybody can cultivate better perception skills.

How You Can Become More Wedded to Reality

You can become more wedded to reality by first assessing data or information the way a pollster does. Pollsters only pay attention to answers and opinions when they're repeated a certain proportion of times or with a certain level of intensity. An issue or opinion is only important to a politician when enough people declare it to be. It reaches critical mass. This is also often the tipping point in mass behavior, consumer taste, and political movements. Steve Case said as much when he recommended looking for underlying messages through repetition and patterns. Be on the lookout for similar responses and connections between and among ideas, much the way a pollster does.

Pattern recognition is invaluable when judging your own behavior. Remember the wisecrack: "If one person calls you a jack-ass—no matter. If a second person calls you a jack-ass, you probably ought to take a look at yourself. And if a third person calls you a jack-ass, guess what? You *are* a jack-ass!"

How Andy Grove of Intel Absorbs Reality

One top-flight entrepreneur who can teach us about information gathering, acute awareness, and, ultimately, survival is Andy Grove, the cofounder of Intel. Back in 2001 I interviewed Grove, then CEO of the microprocessor giant. He is a legend in the annals of technology as well as business. Grove discovered the impurity in silicon (sodium) and thus helped launch the whole computer age. He also cofounded Intel with Gordon Moore and Robert Noyce. Intel is the dominant manufacturer of computer chips and microprocessors—which are the guts of all computers. Grove is known to be as tough as he is brilliant.

He certainly was *testy* the day I interviewed him. Not until the fourth or fifth question did he relax his guard and open up, finally convinced that I had done my homework and that we weren't wasting his time.

I asked this Hungarian-born technologist how, in the early 1980s, he had been able to foresee the rise of the personal computer and had the courage to bet Intel on that prediction. To recognize reality *before* others, Grove stresses open-minded observation, listening, and the absorption of data. "You have to immerse yourself like a sponge into the environment and make yourself available to be influenced by people who want to influence you, who *need* to influence you . . . so each of these decisions properly has to be preceded by a period of absorption, 'listening,' if you wish," he said.[5]

Note that Grove stresses that there are people in your path who have information for you, people to whom you might not typically turn. These people are in a position to see what you cannot see, and because what they know is important or otherwise unknown, they feel a *need* to communicate with you. This need stems from their sense that their knowledge is telling, disturbing, or simply doesn't fit with the beliefs you or your organization has. These individuals may be new to you, far down the organizational ladder, or naturally reticent, but they are agitated because they have information that is salient.

How You Can Become More Realistic

Here are several tips from Andy Grove on how to better recognize reality and thus better grapple with life's big mysteries, questions, and dilemmas:

Don't dispute the data. Make your argument based on data.

If you don't have enough data, collect more.

Conduct experiments in the marketplace to test your thinking and solutions.

Pay extra attention to those who offer conflicting views and incongruous facts.

Like Andy Grove, the good among the great are well aware of their own ignorance so they stay within their areas of competence. They're realistic, even humble about the breadth of their knowledge and skill, which paradoxically makes them more able than most. Simply put, they know their circle of competence and that outside it, they have blind spots. We *all* have blind spots. The best among us also recognize humankind's vast ignorance. Best put by medical researcher Matthias Nahrendorf as quoted in the August 4, 2009 *New York Times*, "The more you learn, the more you realize that we're just scratching on the surface of life. We don't know the whole story about anything."[6]

Paradoxically, this can make the wisest among us more open to fantastic notions and ideas. And why wouldn't it, when what we don't know is so much greater than what we do know. Furthermore, the good among the great recognize that many of the ideas, mores, and wisdom of a generation ago have been abandoned. Just watch an episode of *Mad Men*. The capable realists among us also recognize that so much more is possible as humankind gains ever more knowledge.

Be Efficiently Perceptive

Maslow posits that the psychologically healthiest people not only get it more often than the rest of us, but they understand others and circumstances more *efficiently*—meaning not only faster, but also in less time and with less effort. Maslow called this capacity "an unusual ability to detect the spurious, the fake, and the dishonest personality, and in general to judge people correctly and efficiently."[7]

Indeed, Maslow writes that superior powers of perception make *all of your thinking improve:* "This superiority in the perception of reality eventuates in a superior ability to reason, to perceive the truth, to come to conclusions, to be logical, and to be cognitively efficient in general."[8]

In a way, dedicated realists have minds that are in shape when it comes to reception and perception, as well as analysis and decision making. Their thinking is leaner, more productive, more focused, and thus even prescient. These are critical reasons that they achieve so much—they not only make better, more nuanced choices, they do so with less effort and always looking forward.

Take a Child's-Eye View

What's counterintuitive about these very objective, sophisticated observers of, and practitioners within, reality is that they are often more childlike in their assessment of daily life. Their take on people and events is fresher and less conventional. The rest of us tend to repeat what others are saying. These individuals often have their very own take on people and circumstances. Their language comes across as unaffected.

Maslow compares the best among us to children whose perceptions aren't yet jaded by social conventions. They "are like the child in the fable who saw that the Emperor had no clothes on. These people can see the fresh, the raw, the concrete."[9] Childlike does not mean childish. The last thing these individuals are is naïve or silly.

In addition, the best human beings have other personality traits that make them more childlike and more original in their assessments: As we've learned in prior chapters, they are more experiential, they resist conventional thinking, they have more integrity, and thus they can be more spontaneous and expressive. All these traits add up to an unguarded nature that seems childlike.

How You Can Recognize Changing Reality

Another reason that the good among the great assess the world more clearly and efficiently is because they recognize that reality isn't fixed. Everything is changing, always, so they often test their own assumptions. They're not only receptive to information that challenges their own thinking, unlike the rest of us, they actually look for it. Warren Buffett and Charlie Munger make a point of challenging and *abandoning* at least one of their long-cherished investing assumptions every year.

When there is a pattern to the feedback or to the results that they're getting, especially if it's negative—they pay particular attention. As the physicist and Nobel Laureate Richard Feynman liked to say, "Don't fool yourself, and remember that you're the easiest person to fool."[10] This goes for everyone, including the high and mighty, particularly for those who insist that they're all-knowing—namely, tyrants. And because reality under tyranny is usually a twisted and distorted thing, the acute observer must find truth in strange places, such as humor.

Back in the late 1970s, the Moscow bureau chief for the *New York Times* was Hedrick Smith. He wrote a great book called *The Russians*. The best part was that he included many of the jokes that Russians told each other. These gags were very often at the leadership's expense and gave you a window into Soviet life and thought. One wisecrack was "We pretend to work . . . and they pretend to pay us." Had our brilliant Kremlinologists spent as much time listening to the jokes as they did the propaganda, we'd have known that the Soviet system was a house of cards.

More Realists

What would you give to know the single most important factor in the spectacular success of Warren Buffett and Charlie Munger? What if that factor could be distilled to one personality trait that they learned and continue to hone—a trait that you too could learn, one that could radically improve your understanding of yourself, the world, your choices, and thus your entire life?

You can.

In *Poor Charlie's Almanack*, a book about and by Munger, Buffett tells a story about how Munger was once cornered by an attractive woman at a dinner party. This woman asked Munger to boil down the secret of their success to one word. Buffett said that Munger could have given her a speech on the subject but she insisted on just one word. Ultimately, Munger spat out the word, "Rational!"[11]

Munger also says that one of the qualities he and Buffett always look for in CEOs is superior "reality recognition."[12]

In other words, reality is a slippery thing. Our impression of what's going on is just that, an impression. But so many of us, even the most successful people, do not have a consistently good grip on reality. Why? Because being wedded to reality does not just require smarts or hard work. It also requires psychological health, some courage, and objectivity. Objectivity from your own thoughts and emotions requires knowing *who* you are and *what* you're capable of. Does this seem like an overstatement? No less than Scott Peck, the late, great psychiatrist and best-selling author of *The Road Less Traveled*, wrote, "Mental health is an ongoing process or dedication to reality at all costs."[13] Echoing Maslow regarding the small percentage of people who appreciate the ever-changing and vague nature of reality, Peck also writes, "Only a relative and fortunate few continue until the moment of death exploring the mystery of reality, ever enlarging and refining and redefining their understanding of the world and what is true."[14]

Many of those who make it to the top lose their edge because they surround themselves with sycophants telling them what they want to hear rather than what's truly happening. Surrounded by flatterers and fawners, they get overblown assessments of their abilities. This overconfidence can lead to underestimating the competition and taking on too much responsibility and risk. Or, these leaders are difficult personalities who can't keep the best, most realistic talent around them. Their overblown perceptions of themselves make them insufferable egotists. Their insecurities often make them hierarchical, so they're more apt to disregard information from lower rungs of their organizations. The high achievers who are also healthy beings have longevity at the top, and a key reason is their tenacious dedication to reality.

It's important to remember that not all leaders or high achievers are great human beings. Maslow theorized that great human beings (those who spend much of their lives maximizing their potential as individuals as well as serving others) are perhaps only 1 percent of the general population. To be sure, there are more great human beings among high achievers—from what I can gather, I'd guess maybe 5 to 10 percent, and among longstanding high achievers, maybe 30 percent. The bulk of those at the top of society are still very talented, very focused, very driven individuals but they just lack many of the traits in this book.

Nevertheless, the point here is that being a hard-core realist is the trait that really matters in terms of achieving earthly success: money, power, and fame. Learning and practicing the skills to be diligently realistic will open doors to so much knowledge about yourself, as well as others and the world, that it will catapult you forward toward your goals.

Live in the World of Nature

Maslow goes on to say that self-actualizing people "live far more in the real world of nature than the verbalized world of concepts, abstractions, expectations, beliefs, and stereotypes that most people confuse with the real world."[15] For most of us, our thinking skews our perceptions. Our emotional baggage gets in the way of our having clarity because often we only hear what we want to hear, or we jump to conclusions because we're lazy or biased. People with healthy psyches focus on specifics. They see what's in front of them. They're highly aware of detail, pattern, and incongruity. And they don't have to strain to be that way. They can see what's in front of them because they're less focused on themselves.

Before you get discouraged about your own perception skills, don't worry. No one is born a flawless observer. Even the most capable among us have to work at it. Those who assess the world more clearly and efficiently work hard to get good information, routinely checking their perceptions against their own preferences and predilections. They gather wise people around them and solicit feedback on their perceptions and reactions. If they can do all these things, so can you.

When you fail to achieve one of your goals, it's very likely because you didn't see or sense the problem or circumstance clearly at the beginning. As a result, you didn't estimate your abilities, commitment, or response commensurately. The failure doesn't mean that "it wasn't meant to be." If your perceptions are as true as they can be, and you are as true to yourself as you can be, then more in your life will work out as *you* intend, not as some nebulous force intends.

Life is not meant to be lived on autopilot. The most capable among us are far more in control of their own destinies than the least capable. Now you can be too, though reaching your goals is going to require a lot of honesty, sensitivity, and courage on your part. To get you started, let's check in again with the masterminds of the Berkshire Hathaway corporation.

Buffett and Munger consider "reality recognition" a valuable and lifelong pursuit. For instance, Munger is a big fan of biographies, particularly those of scientists, because he wants to know how these individuals perceive the world. Scientists, of course, are wedded to the "scientific method," which requires rigorous testing and measurement, double-blind studies, and efficaciousness. Groundbreaking scientists challenge the consensus thinking.

Don't Believe Everything You Think

Philosophically and psychologically healthy people like Buffett and Munger don't just accept the way they think and believe. They constantly test their own assumptions and ideas, their financial forecasts, and their assessments of others, and they do so against rigorous mental checklists. They also invert the questions and problems they're studying. They measure results, seek the opinions of respected third parties, and carefully gauge their own and others' reactions.

So, it should be no surprise that Warren Buffett and Charlie Munger have foreseen and warned the rest of us about nearly every financial calamity America has experienced in the last thirty years, including the dot-com, subprime mortgage, and derivatives busts. They warned us that Fannie Mae and Freddie Mac were taking on too much risk. As early as 1982, Buffett wrote to members of Congress citing the inherent risk of derivative contracts (a kind of side bet on other financial instruments). In his 2002 letter to shareholders, Buffett called derivatives "toxic" and said that they were "time bombs" that could eventually cause a financial disaster. This was at a time when many commentators argued that derivatives reduced systemic risk.

Have a "Superior Relationship with Reality"

Maslow writes that the self-actualizing "have a superior relationship with reality," which enables them to distinguish "the fresh, concrete, and ideographic from the generic, abstract, and categorized . . . They are therefore far more apt to perceive what is there rather than their own wishes, hopes, fears, anxieties, their own theories and beliefs, or those of their cultural group."[16] There's a lot in that quote to digest, some of which we'll tackle in later chapters. However, the thrust of Maslow's thinking, and what I've found among mega-achievers, is that to be realistic, you need to perceive each day, each person, everything very specifically and concretely. That's how you see things in a fresher way. The good among the great focus on specifics. They see what's in front of them. They're more awake to each moment, each person, and each event with all their subtle, yet telling details. Those who see more clearly and efficiently delight in observation. Thus they see, hear, smell, and feel a lot more than the rest of us.

Be a Well, Not a Fountain

So how do we absorb reality? Grove and Case urge us to develop keen listening and observation skills. For most of us, that first and foremost means *shutting up*. Notice the next time you're at a cocktail party whether you or anyone else is truly listening and responding, or whether they're just waiting to talk about their opinions, their thoughts, their children, themselves.

Meryl Streep said, "Listening is everything. Listening is the whole deal. It's where you learn everything."[17]

Shelly Lazarus, long-time CEO and now chairman of advertising giant Ogilvy & Mather Worldwide, told me that one of the best expressions she's ever heard is that those who don't listen "have very small ears. And now I can sit across from people and their ears shrink as I listen to them."[18]

If you're a good listener, you'll make more friends—being heard is flattering. And if you're really empathizing, you'll get away from *your own repetitive internal chatter*. The healthiest individuals are less self-involved. This not only gives them a clearer, more objective perception of others and reality, it makes them better listeners as well as more outwardly focused and more problem focused. (We'll discuss this further in chapters 13 and 14.)

Being a good listener is not easy. Even data-gathering professionals have to work at it. Most interviewers, even some of the best, talk too much and listen too little.

Be Precise and Concise

Learning to condense your conversation is another way to talk less, and thus listen more. But brevity isn't easy when it comes to talking or writing. In television news, the old joke among writers is "It's not hard to write *well*. It's hard to write *short!*" When I interviewed Andy Grove, I was struck by the concision as well as the precision of his language. Precise thinkers speak with a disciplined care that makes them more discerning in their thinking, ideas, conclusions, counsel, everything. Silence can also be a very powerful exclamation point. It's amazing how few people use it to good effect. When you want to make yourself very clear, offer your thought in one sentence, and then stop talking. You'll be surprised how well you get your point across.

If you are deliberate and pithy with your speech, you will be more respected and more respectful of the facts (and hopefully of others). This will require that you be more rigorous with your memory, data, analysis, opinion, and judgment. Doing so will sharpen your thinking and further assist you in being more wedded to reality.

Consider the Source

Once you develop the habit of talking less and listening, observing and absorbing more, then direct your heightened awareness to higher-quality sources. Do what objective journalists do, and "consider the source." Listen and trust those whom you respect and admire; discount the rest.

The Proof Is in the Proceeds

Finally, remember this: the proof is not in the pudding. It's not even "in the eating" of the pudding, as the old expression correctly goes. Proof of the quality of your life and your choices is in the living. The proceeds of your sensitivity, receptivity, perceptions, assessments of reality, and ultimately, your effort and choices is reflected every day in the quality of your life. The success of your attitudes and behaviors depends on your assessment of what's truly going on. Your ability to recognize reality can be judged in how well you're living and how much money, respect, and love you're getting and giving. In other words, judge virtually all aspects of your life—your relationships, your career, your bank account—by *results*. And your results depend first on how well you perceive reality.

Takeaways

Reality is a slippery thing. The wisest among us make better reality recognition a lifelong effort. Also, being realistic is the *big* trait when it comes to succeeding in our materialistic, cutthroat society. The other eighteen traits are also valuable in gathering material success, but they are important for emotional sustenance, tranquility, contentment, and spiritual evolution as well.

- ✓ The first step toward wisdom is the recognition of your ignorance.
- ✓ Resist the urge to always have an answer; practice saying, "I don't know."
- ✓ Don't exaggerate or understate. Precision in language will tighten your thinking and improve your judgment.
- ✓ Think of "absorbing," not just hearing or learning information.
- ✓ Don't make snap judgments. Use analysis as well as intuition.
- ✓ Resist categorization. Every individual and circumstance is unique.
- ✓ Assess like a pollster: Argue using data, don't argue *with* the data. Pay attention to information when its occurrence reaches a certain threshold.
- ✓ Don't rely on experts alone. Do, and trust, your *own* analysis.
- ✓ Seek "reality checks" from those you admire.
- ✓ Remember Maslow's advice: "To avoid disillusionment with human nature, we must first give up our illusions about it."[19]
- ✓ Remember that the proof is in the proceeds.

Chapter 9

··

Chill Out!

TRAIT: *LAID BACK*

See the world in a grain of sand,
And a heaven in a wildflower,
Hold infinity in the palm of my hand
And eternity in an hour.

—WILLIAM BLAKE

OVER THE YEARS, I'VE met a number of people who exhibit remarkable calmness in the face of risk and uncertainty and fear. Andy Grove of Intel, whom you'll get to know in chapter 14, is one. But of all those I've interviewed, Melinda Cunningham stands out because her laid-back nature is a key reason she's still alive. And as a young mother she had to face the terrifying mystery we all face—death. When Melinda was only thirty-one years old and still nursing her baby daughter, she was diagnosed with full-blown AIDS.

Monogamous and never an intravenous drug user, Melinda still doesn't know how she contracted the virus. Remarkably, she doesn't waste time trying to guess who gave it to her. "You just can't blame people," she said. Echoing Rachel Walton's refusal to hold a grudge in chapter 2, Melinda went on, "You get bitter if you try to obsess about where it came from. Life is too short. You can't dwell on those things."[1]

Of course you can. Many of us nurse the wounds of life as if they owned us, trotting them out as evidence against those who've done us wrong. But people who assess the world clearly and efficiently realize a couple of important truths: that dwelling on wrongs hurts the victim more than the perpetrator and that life moves on even if we don't. This objectivity (chapter 6) and realism (chapter 8) leads them to the fact that life isn't fair and that we waste precious time demanding that it ought to be. Melinda demonstrated a third trait—appreciation—when she choked up a bit and declared, "It was about time something bad happened. I had an incredibly blessed life. I've been so lucky. Basically, I've had nothing bad happen to me until this. It's a matter of odds."[2]

A laid-back nature can also make the good among the great come across as shockingly matter-of-fact. Since Melinda had to suddenly face her own mortality, you might expect her to seek solace in organized religion or at least some form of faith. But she said, "I don't have faith. I really don't believe in an afterlife. I can see how people do, but me personally, I don't. Death does not scare me because it's an end. It's over."[3]

People with strong, healthy psyches, like Melinda, remain unruffled by the events that rattle the average person. This chapter looks closely at why and how the psychologically healthiest people cope with the stresses, adversities, and setbacks that often undo the rest of us. How do the best and strongest among us cultivate their resilience? How do they face the unknown with courage and calm—indeed, even excitement?

Maslow's Take

A calm objectivity, even detachment from one's own existence, is detailed in chapter 6 and springs from the autonomy that these individuals possess. The combination gives them a deep well of resilience. Think of Nelson Mandela enduring twenty-seven years in prison and then forgiving his captors upon emerging.

Maslow writes, "This independence of environment means a relative stability in the face of hard knocks, blows, deprivations, frustrations, and the like. These people can maintain a relative serenity in the midst of circumstances that would drive other people to suicide; they also have been described as self-contained."[4] I would call them self-sufficient.

This independence of environment also gives the good among the great just enough distance from their circumstances that they can see and accept life's paradoxes. They are drawn to rather than repelled by its mysteries. As Abraham Maslow puts it, "They do not cling to the familiar, nor is their quest for the truth a catastrophic need for certainty, definiteness and order." He goes on, "Thus it comes that doubt, tentativeness, uncertainty, with the consequent necessity for abeyance of decision, which is for most a torture, can be for some a pleasantly stimulating challenge, a high spot in life rather than a low."[5]

In other words, those situations we've all been in that are uncomfortable because of a lack of information or certainty are exciting rather than unnerving to those with the best temperaments. Indeed, Maslow notes that even in those circumstances, "They find it easy to be aloof, reserved, and also calm and serene; thus it becomes possible for them to take personal misfortunes without reacting violently as the ordinary person does."[6] Melinda

Cunningham, for example, doesn't spend time questioning her lot in life, cursing the heavens, or wondering how or why she got AIDS. Instead, she accepts her lot. She then goes about doing what she can do rather than focusing on what she can't. She doesn't ask, Why me? when she knows the next question very well could be, Why not me? Taking a page from the book of optimism, she turns to see the good, the love, the many blessings that she has been given.

In the summer of 1994, when her estimated life span was measured in months rather than years, I asked her if her excitement about life was tempered by her prognosis. Melinda shook her head, "No, not at all. I don't look at it that way. I value life so much more now. I used to wish my life away, always looking forward to the future. 'Oh, I'm going skiing in two weeks,' or 'Oh, I'm going to Canada this summer.' You don't enjoy day to day when you're always looking ahead. Without a doubt, I've started to live in the present so much more. I make a conscious effort to enjoy each day."[7]

Many of us would fret and fall into a deep depression if we knew we had only months to live. This kind of pessimistic need for order and answers can skew all kinds of critical decision making, even if we do not face a life-threatening illness.

Indeed, many of us hate uncertainty so much that we'd rather believe something erroneous than simply accept that we do not know. That's one reason most of us don't like change and why we love predictions. We'd rather hang our futures on some soothsayer than settle for the unknown.

How many times have you heard friends or acquaintances declare their predictions about a football game, the stock market, a friend's marriage, or the next election? On the financial news channels, the data streams are marvelous and the news reports strong, but certain shows are filled with financial forecasters who will tell you where a stock or the Dow will be in three months, six months, a year. Pick a date, and they'll give you a number. It's a fool's game. Forecasting not only gives you (almost certainly) false information but also gives you false assurance when you ought to be on guard. Get the data, but discount the forecasts.

And remember as Maslow wrote "that for healthy people the unknown is not frightening."[8] Indeed, they don't push unrealistically for definiteness and order. "They can be, when the total objective situation calls for it, comfortably disorderly, sloppy, anarchic, chaotic, vague, doubtful, uncertain, indefinite, approximate, inexact, or inaccurate (all at certain moments in science, art, or life in general, quite desirable)."[9]

One example of this trait is that many, many times my best friends will allow their children to make chaos in their homes for the sheer fun of it—water-balloon fights, packs of dogs chasing each other amidst guests, loud music and dancing—often disrupting the most carefully planned dinner parties. The result can be an explosion of exuberance and spontaneity that makes everything delightfully uncertain.

Lest you think that those who assess the world clearly and efficiently don't worry or suffer when hit with bad news, it's important to note that Melinda has not ignored or hidden from the reality of HIV. While death doesn't frighten her, the process of dying an agonizing death certainly does: "Dying is scary—terrifying. That without a doubt scares me the most. Becoming sick, becoming frail and helpless, that's horrible."[10]

Indeed, in the mid-1990s, shortly after she was diagnosed, Melinda would often lie awake at night. "The first year I couldn't sleep at all," she admitted. "A big part of that was having a child. That makes it much more difficult to deal with everything. If it's just you you're worried about, that's one thing. But if you have a child, you think, 'I won't see her grow up. I won't see her graduate from high school. I won't see her get married.' When I didn't feel like I'd live that long, that was what would keep me up at night."[11]

Remember Mary Cunningham from chapter 6, our exemplar for Maslow's trait of objectivity and detachment? Mary is Melinda's mother. One might think that any parent would panic upon finding out that her daughter has the HIV virus. True to form, Mary responded with poise and objectivity.

"She was very calm," Melinda said, even though in March 1994, a doctor in Colorado told Mary that Melinda had six months to live. "Her answer was, 'What can we do?'" The whole Cunningham family remained calm. After the initial shock, they set about finding a more proactive doctor, got Melinda enrolled in a groundbreaking UCLA study, and procured an experimental "cocktail" of something no one had heard of: protease inhibitors. Melinda was one of the first people to get this lifesaving serum. Fortunately, she had one of the mildest forms of HIV, and her body responded well to the treatment. Her laid-back demeanor kept her focused on the present and future. It's been seventeen years since her diagnosis, and blood tests haven't shown the HIV virus in Melinda's blood for several years. She is a healthy, happy mother of a thriving teenage girl.

How You Can Be More Laid Back

You can be more laid back by first accepting your ignorance. Those who assess the world more clearly and efficiently, no matter how successful they are, are better all-around choice makers because they're never too sure of themselves, their capabilities, or their situations. As one of my most successful friends put it, "You've got to be comfortable with the 'gray' in life." This means most of our options, not just ethical issues, don't appear as black-or-white choices. First of all, people are flawed and not always trustworthy. Also, often we don't have enough information. We're forced to make decisions based on limited or conflicting data. That uncertainty makes us anxious—so instead of gathering more data or finding ways to hedge our bets or postponing choices, we convince ourselves that we know more than we do. This is not so for the temperamentally strong.

As Maslow puts it, for them, "the unknown is not frightening, they do not have to spend any time laying the ghost, whistling past the cemetery, or otherwise protecting themselves against imagined dangers." Most of us are so uncomfortable with the unknown, so much so that we mistake assumptions for perceptions and jump to conclusions to fill in gaps in our knowledge. In Maslow's words, "They do not neglect the unknown, or deny it, or run away from it, or try to make believe it is really known."[12]

Laid-back individuals remind themselves how little they know, how little we as a culture and as a species know, and furthermore how everything is constantly changing so that even those things they do know won't be valid for long.

Sound scary? Think of it as stimulating.

Just as the most laid-back among us embrace the unknown in life, they also recognize the "factitude" of specific, real, concrete things rather than trusting their own abstract ideas about them. As Maslow writes, they "live far more in the real world of nature than the verbalized world of concepts, abstractions, expectations, beliefs, and stereotypes that most people confuse with the real world."[13]

So spend more time in nature. Think and behave more like a wild animal with cubs in your care. Be alert. Be prepared. Risk is everywhere, but you can minimize it—this knowledge can give you real calm.

Here's another paradox to accept: the more you recognize that you don't know, the harder you work for good information, and thus, the more you will truly know.

Resisting predictions and assumptions, discounting your own theories and those of others and simply accepting how little can be known, is important for many reasons. You'll be more open to new ideas, and you'll also be a better negotiator.

A big part of life is getting what you want through negotiation, and one part of a successful negotiation is not predicting or guessing the other side's motivations, reasoning, or next move. Of course, you should gather all the valid data that you can about your counterparts and their wants and needs. But you must actively resist assuming too much or guessing at their next steps, demands, or limits. Those kinds of suppositions are usually faulty, and worse, they tilt your own behavior and responses—almost always incorrectly. Your speculation not only infects your thinking and actions but can also give you false comfort, making you more likely to overreach.

On the other hand, if you're able to accept the limits of your knowledge, you become more agnostic about the outcome of the negotiation. That helps you relax.

The wisest people gather good data on their counterparts and make incremental moves, taking each step based on the best information they can find. They do their own analysis within their area of competence and develop a clear sense of value, an honest assessment of how much they want and need, and a conservative guess as to how much the other side wants and needs to get a deal done. Then they resist overreaching and let the chips fall where they may. Usually, those chips fall in a pretty good place. Indeed, these people's missteps are few. And the surprises the good among the great encounter tend to be on the upside. Negotiate that way a few times and you'll get more laid back too!

Melinda Cunningham—as well as other exceptional individuals like her—doesn't dwell on the past or what is irreversible. She focuses on today. She now spends time educating others about protecting themselves from HIV. She pays more attention to what's truly valuable. And she doesn't dwell on petty issues. As Abraham Maslow puts it, "Such people live customarily in the widest possible frame of reference. They seem never to get so close to the trees that they fail to see the forest. They work within a framework of values that are broad and not petty, universal and not local, and in terms of a century rather than the moment . . . The result is a certain serenity and lack of worry over immediate concerns that make life easier not only for themselves but for all who are associated with them."[14]

In other words, serenity—stepping back and being more philosophical about your life and the bad things that happen to you—will "make life easier" not only for you, "but for all who are associated with" you.

This combination of traits—deep self-awareness, better recognition of reality, strong moral moorings, and loving relationships—can make you calmer in the face of uncertainty. And because the good among the great are not bothered by the natural uncertainty of life, they don't waste valuable time feeling frustrated, wronged, or impotent—another reason that they get more accomplished! Instead, these good and strong souls accept and even enjoy the mysteries all around us, recognizing that they make the experience of life more exciting.

One Buddhist teaching suggests that life is a lot like falling off a cliff. Some people live their lives in terror, clutching at every rock and branch on the way down. Others accept their mortality and make the most of the time they have—especially since they don't really know how much time they have or where their fall may ultimately land them.

Takeaways

Being laid back is a marvelous by-product of several other traits, such as being realistic, autonomous, loving, and detached. Being laid back, despite all the mystery as well as the trouble and trauma that we all face, will make life easier for you and those around you.

✓ Relish the present instead of questioning past choices and events or rushing toward "what's next."

✓ Resist the need for certainty, definiteness, and order. These rarely if ever exist.

✓ Resist the tendency to predict. Many forecasts are born of fear and discomfort, not knowledge.

✓ Cultivate patience when gathering information. For example, when discussing important issues, wait for others to give their impressions and conclusions before you speak.

✓ When negotiating, fight the urge to make assumptions. Make your moves with the best information you can attain, and then let the chips fall where they may.

✓ Accept your mortality and that of those you love. Accept that you or they may die or be incapacitated at any time, and make the most of the time and choices you have.

....

Chapter 10

Tap-Dance to Work

TRAIT: *PERFORMANCE AND PROCESS ORIENTED*

We work to become, not to acquire.

—ELBERT HUBBARD

IN THE SPRING OF 2010, two consummate artists staged a bold experiment. Damian Smith, a principal dancer with the San Francisco Ballet Company, paired with Muriel Maffre, one of the great ballerinas of our time, to create a marvelous piece of art. But there was no stage, no grand opera hall. Damian and Muriel worked with a composer and choreographer to create a series of early stage rehearsals in a San Francisco storefront. Instead of a performance, passersby got a peek at two perspiration-soaked ballet stars presenting their *process* for public consumption.

Muriel Maffre is the poster child for process as well as performance. An unusually tall ballerina at six-foot-four en pointe, this cerebral French artist has defied expectations and become an international sensation. Her career has been defined by many successes. She danced for seventeen years with the San Francisco Ballet as a principal, and upon retiring from the company in 2008, she received the highest honor a French artist can attain when she was named Chevalier de l'Ordre des Arts et des Lettres by the French Ministry of Culture. And yet for Maffre, all of this is secondary. She dances because she is deeply in love with the process, not the honors, the adulation, or the applause.

"It is very gratifying for me to deemphasize the moment of the performance," she said in her thick but elegant accent, "which can be very beautiful and very rich and intense . . . but also, when you are a perfectionist, the performance can be disappointing. By bringing focus and value to the process, I found a place where I could be gratified at all times with my work."[1]

For those lucky enough to work with Maffre, the process is a glorious if intimidating exercise in preparation—the deconstruction of steps, her rigorous focus on the "honesty" of every gesture, and the fierce discipline she brings to each rehearsal. In 2004, a younger member of the corps at SFB, named Garren Price Scribner, came to Maffre with his own crisis of confidence, saying "I'm having a breakdown." She looked at him coolly and said, "It's not a breakdown. It's a break*through*."[2]

Maffre explained her devotion to process as an intensely personal revelation. "Process can be just the digging deeper and deeper every time . . . It's also cumulative, building something, not 'the performance thing,' not showing you at your best every time and not having that goal necessarily. That can be *vain*." These are striking words from a woman working in a world defined by vanity, presentation, and the pursuit of perfection. After all, ballet is a grandly constructed illusion where effortless grace is the goal. And yet Maffre strives to strip the polish. "There is the luster which is actually a barrier to seeing what is really authentic. There is a projection, there is a forcing—*forcing* to have you like it. It's selling something."[3]

In those three sentences, Maffre articulates five traits that are shared among great, grounded human beings. Not only is Maffre acutely aware of and sensitive to others—namely the audience (empathic), she also has a deep respect for them (egalitarian). She is as intent on the joy of creating a ballet as she is on performing it (creative and process as well as performance oriented). She also sees through the artifice (realistic). And finally, she is profoundly independent and true to herself (autonomous). Combining those traits with her talent adds up to an authenticity that is *riveting*.

Damian Smith, who has frequently been Maffre's dance partner over the years, said "You can have the whole San Francisco Ballet leaping in high costume on one side of the stage while Muriel simply walks onto the other, and the audience will watch *her*."[4]

That's an amazing power from a dancer who was not even supposed to dance. Growing up in a small village west of Paris, Maffre started performing on an outdoor tennis court because the area had no theater. At the age of nine, she was accepted at the revered Paris Opera. But by sixteen, she had grown tall—a formidable five-foot-ten. "I had a very formal education in ballet at the Paris Opera, and I think it made me very, very self-conscious." The incessant criticism she received is what made her so self-conscious. Ultimately, her instructors dismissed this prodigy, telling her "You are a beautiful plant. But you can't dance."[5]

But even if the arbiters of ballet rejected this lanky artist, the art itself wooed her. "I fell in love with ballet. I fell in love with the physical aspect of ballet, and then through that it took something away and brought something in. What it took away—was kind of this ability to relate easily through words, through normal means of communication."[6]

So Maffre turned inward and focused on meaning as much as technique, what she calls "a quality of intention" for each and every movement. Despite her detractors, she created a life and career "by really developing something that was completely in tune with who I was and cultivating that out." That's a perfect rendition of the value of self-discovery and a self-directed life (chapter 1). Also, what irony! By forcing Maffre to find more than physical perfection, her detractors diverted her toward her singular talent.[7]

Developing that talent has required a day-to-day rigor. "It is important because it's about discovering something new every time," Maffre said. "It's about fine-tuning . . . about being this archeologist. You dig deeper and find more because it is discovering something new and bringing new ideas to the table each time."[8]

For Maffre, the dancer and the person, digging deeper is about finding the most genuine way of communicating ideas, emotions, and, most profoundly, who she is. Authenticity is so powerful onstage because, as she said, "It's *you*! It's the truth. It's who you are for real."[9]

The reason Maffre finds dance so profound and audiences find her mere presence so compelling is because every movement, from a stately arabesque to the flicker of a finger, transmits a message of utter sincerity. When asked why it is so important that every gesture be honest, she replied, "I find that there is more depth when there is intention behind a movement because it connects to the roots, *your* roots."[10] (See chapter 1 for much more on this trait of self-awareness, self-acceptance, and autonomy.)

In life, most of us are judged by what we deliver, not how we deliver it. This chapter aims to describe how the best among us not only deliver great products, services, and performances but also take great pride and joy in the *doing*. Of course, by making your process joyous, you have a much better shot at being a top performer. It means creating a daily routine tailored to your talents, needs, and, most of all, wants. Instead of making your work merely a means to an end, make it an end in and of itself, and the other ends will very likely take care of themselves.

Maslow's Take

Abraham Maslow wrote that great human beings clearly distinguish between means and ends, between preparation and achievement. But they also find delight in their work. They are "somewhat more likely to appreciate for its own sake, and in an absolute way, the doing itself; they can enjoy for its own sake the getting to some place as well as the arriving."[11]

This is wonderful because it supports the notion that you *ought* to do what you want to do, which is the gist of chapter 1 on autonomy. Even more compelling, the best among us invert that premise—they want to do what they ought to do. We'll get into this trait of responsibility or dutifulness in much more detail in chapter 14, but as Maslow puts it, among the best human beings, "desires are in excellent accord with reason. Duty cannot be contrasted with pleasure nor work with play when duty is pleasure, when work is play, and the person doing his duty and being virtuous is simultaneously seeking his pleasure and being happy."[12]

What an affirmation for finding and doing what you love!

Maslow goes on to state that some people also possess the ability to "make out the most trivial and routine activity as intrinsically enjoyable game or dance or play."[13] An analysis of Muriel Maffre's story provides us with the perfect example. For many performers the rehearsal process can be tedious and trying. Their moment comes when they're onstage, in front of an audience. That's where they rise to the occasion and shine; everything that comes before is merely a series of steps to get them to that place.

But for Maffre, the getting there is intrinsically enjoyable. In fact, it's *more* enjoyable.

Maslow writes that self-actualizing individuals don't look outside themselves for gratification. Their basic needs are the same as everyone else's: physiological (food and shelter), then safety (security and stability), then social (love and belonging), and finally esteem (respect and standing). The strongest and healthiest psyches have had these needs satisfied. They then focus on self-actualization and on reaching their potential. For each person that is a unique and compelling motivation: "What humans *can* be, they *must* be. They must be true to their own nature."[14]

These strong and fortunate individuals don't base their own joy or satisfaction on the approval of others or on rewards from others. Instead, they look within themselves to develop what Maslow called "their own talents, capacities, potentialities, and the like."[15] After years of hard work, sweat, and criticism, Maffre excels at doing exactly that. Now, no longer a dancer with the San Francisco Ballet, she is teaching at Stanford, doing guest appearances for a variety of dance companies, working on her master's degree in museum studies, and working as a curator at the Richmond Museum in northern California. Through all of this she is doing what she feels compelled to do: communicate emotion, knowledge, and honesty through art.

How You Can Become More Process Oriented

I believe each of us is born with an innate desire to both make our mark on the world and delight in the doing. However, we all face a world of teachers, examiners, and bosses who are constantly demanding products and performances—proof of our work and worth. Your defense against the bean counters of your productivity is finding what delights you despite what you produce. Then you may champion process as well as performance every day.

If you want a work process that is pleasurable, you must start by doing something you like—or better yet, love. Maffre always loved dance despite the strain, pain, and rejection. Her passion for her day-to-day work has fulfilled the promise of her true and individual potential. This fulfillment isn't possible just in the world of dance or art. It's equally possible in most fields.

If you want to be accomplished, and even more, if you want to be joyous regardless of your level of achievement, find what excites you every day. It doesn't have to be the same thing that excited you ten years ago; in fact, it's very likely that your preferred routine will evolve throughout your life, as it should to reflect your inner self—whoever that self is at any given moment. If you find what excites you, then your process is likely to be joyous.

In the same line of thinking, Warren Buffett advises business school students to choose work that they want to do and to choose bosses and colleagues whom they like and admire. Waiting years to enjoy your work, he warns, is akin to waiting until you're old to have sex.

In his 2009 shareholders' letter, Buffett wrote that he still "tap dances to the office every day." That's being in love with the process. If you shift to a job that delights you every day, you will also increase the odds that you'll succeed, even in a field where you have little to no training. When you're excited to work, life becomes less about goals and more about what's right in front of you. As the great investor also said, "We enjoy the process far more than the proceeds."[16]

Unfortunately, we're often taught from a young age that the only thing that matters is achieving the goal. It's part of living in competitive market economies. Western and American cultures in particular emphasize the same message: results matter, winning is the most important thing or, even worse, the *only* thing. From grammar school to graduate school, what matters are credentials, not the day-to-day joy of living, serving others, or creating.

The irony is that so many people who excel at getting are not great when it comes to being. Many, maybe most, of the great business and political achievers whom I've encountered are this way. They have an incessant focus on the next goal, a higher rung, a fatter wallet. The minority, the kind of individual whom I'm focusing on in this book, are also good individuals. Their achievements are most often simply derivative of their joyous pursuit of what they care about. It's important to recognize that many good, strong, giving people choose to not be highly recognized or rewarded achievers. They're great parents and family members. They're great friends and community leaders. They're great in quiet ways. They know who they are. If you know them, you know who they are. They're the people you admire, and one critical reason you admire them is that they move to their own music.

That's how you find the path that's yours—the path that sets you tap-dancing to work every day. "Follow your bliss" is what Joseph Campbell, the late, great professor of comparative religion, used to say. That, he argued, will get you where and who you want to be.[17]

Of course, a statement like "follow your bliss" can seem fanciful when times are tough. However, do not use a bad economy as a reason to forego doing what you truly love to do. The truth is that even when the economy was good, plenty of people who were making good money—lawyers, managers, CEOs—were doing what they didn't want to do. When urged to abandon their high-paying drudgery, they'd often sneer or roll their eyes. No matter how much they longed to change their lives, the money held them back.

In this economy, if you're out of work, then you're free to make a shift. What may seem at first like a devastating loss is also an opportunity. You may be struggling financially; perhaps you're relying on your spouse or the government right now and you feel ashamed or unworthy. But look at the bright side: you have a chance to explore what is internally compelling. What moves you? Where would you prefer to live? What sort of work would make you excited to get out of bed in the morning?

Of course, you can't forget about feeding your offspring or keeping a roof over your head. So, you have to plan. And if you have a family, it's probably not time to pack up and head to Hawaii because you've always wanted to surf. Start small. You can find a dozen ways to tap into what matters most to you. If you don't have a dream job, then start by paying attention to your daydreams. Listen to your heart and recognize the little things that would make your daily routine more joyous, calm, focused, and productive.

How You Can Become More Focused on Process

A number of tips come in handy for moving to a mind-set that's process as well as performance oriented. You can start by making your surroundings less media and marketing intensive. Turn off the television; switch off your cell phone. (See chapter 4.)

Spend more time alone. Most people don't value their alone time; in fact, they try to avoid it because they feel lonely or anxious. (See chapter 5.) All the good among the great characters I've known cherish their privacy and relish their solitude. When you quiet the incessant noise in your life and chatter in your mind, you can open up your sensory apparatus and truly see, hear, feel, and experience the world and those around you. You can also be like Maffre and do some internal archeology. Be receptive to be perceptive.

Meditation is also helpful in terms of restructuring the mind and giving you distance from your own thoughts (see chapter 4). Scientific studies have shown that the basic brain structure differs in those who have meditated for a long time compared to those who haven't. Dr. Andrew Weil says that meditation can actually alter the structure of your mind. Weil meditates most days in order to give him "some space from his thoughts."[18] The best bumper sticker I ever saw read "Don't believe everything you think." You're fallible, and a lot of what you think is nonsense.

Calm the internal mind chatter. Alter your routine. Turn off the radio in your car. Hear your thoughts and tune in to those of others. Remember that thought is a social construct. Marleen McDaniel, former CEO of www.women.com and a successful Silicon Valley technology executive told me once that "ideas are in the ether."[19] When she drives home from work, she shuts off the radio to gather them up.

Whatever you feel you want to change or improve, be on the lookout for ways to do more of what you want to do. If you're outwardly focused, if you're problem focused as the good among the great are, then you will be in service to others while you also respect yourself. In a methodical way, move away from what you're sick and tired of and toward what excites you, toward some activity that's more aligned with your heart. Chances are, you'll soon be tap-dancing your way to work.

But first, you've got to strategize, plan, and provision.

Be Prepared

"More important than the will to win is the will to prepare."[20] This is a favorite quote of Charlie Munger.

So much disappointment in life stems from our inability to turn dreams into goals and goals into realities. Often, this is due not to a lack of desire but to a lack of preparation. Preparation requires patient study, organization, and provisioning. Preparation is also about process. If you learn to enjoy and cherish the process of preparation your chances for success skyrocket. Whether we're discussing Muriel Maffre or any of the other leaders whom I've profiled over the years, you'll see that all of them are organized, focused preparers.

Munger is right. Simply wanting and exerting blunt effort for something is not enough. Wanting and working for it is necessary, of course, but in our fiercely competitive schools and workplaces, you have to be more precise: honing your skills, provisioning time and resources economically, and preparing in every detail. Devotion to preparation will vastly improve your final product or performance.

Listen to Your Music

In his research, Maslow points out how children can turn even the dullest work into play. In one experiment, they turned the banal task of transporting books from one set of shelves to another "into a structured and amusing game . . . by doing this according to a certain system or with a certain rhythm."[21] That inner music—what gives you joy, what truly moves you—is what you ought to make your process, just as you did when you were a child.

Takeaways

Carefully delineate and prepare to reach your goals but then work in such a way that you also delight in the doing! Construct your day and your life to suit your wants and needs so that you, like Muriel Maffre, may be more joyous and break through constraints to your potential.

- ✓ Create a daily routine tailored to your wants and talents, not just your needs or the needs of others.
- ✓ Find time each day to tune out the "chattering mind" and tune in to your inner rhythm.
- ✓ Don't believe everything you think.
- ✓ Pay attention to your daydreams, particularly when you drive, shower, and walk. These are times of sensory stimulation and thus open paths to non-analytical wisdom.
- ✓ Be alert to what excites you.
- ✓ Seek and learn to enjoy time alone.
- ✓ Remember what Bill Bradley says, "Feelings are as valuable as thinking."
- ✓ Make your "process" a priority, and the performance will take care of itself.

Part 3

....

Caring and Interacting with Others Effectively

....

Chapter 11

Respect All Souls

TRAIT: *EGALITARIAN*

Can I see another's woe, and not be in sorrow too? Can I see another's grief, and not seek for kind relief?

—WILLIAM BLAKE

IN 2005, A NEWLY minted graduate of Dickinson College headed to the ghetto of New Haven, Connecticut. While many of his friends were backpacking through Europe or netting impressive entry salaries on Wall Street, Andrew Ferguson went to teach sixty-eight underprivileged boys in a broken-down trailer. The roof leaked, the walls had holes punched in them, and the building was condemned at the end of Ferguson's first year. "It should have been condemned my first day."[1]

As a young white man hailing from a life of relative privilege, Ferguson found his job to be a radical experience. All of his students were black and fatherless. Only one had a male authority figure in his life. Ferguson saw suspicion, doubt, and even hatred in the small faces that looked up at him every day. The prospect of connecting with these children in any way, let alone teaching them, was daunting.

About six weeks into the job, Ferguson went to work one day like any other morning. In some ways, his main achievement to that point was simply that he hadn't quit. On that particular day, he happened to be wearing a sweater vest. As he walked in, Quashon, one of the shortest and heaviest ten-year-olds, leapt up and yelled, "Nice fuckin' sweater vest, cracker!"[2]

Although he was shocked, Ferguson kept his cool. And despite never having experienced anything like this, he knew exactly what was going on. "At the school, there's a history of the guys running teachers out," he explained. "And then there's the bigger history of these boys knowing that any male in their life is going to run out. So I knew I was being tested and that this was one of the tests.

"I also knew that they were used to teachers screaming back. My sense is that the teacher never won when that happened. And then my personality—I just don't do that. So I took a deep breath and said, 'Okay.' Once he saw that he wasn't going to get a reaction or provoke some retaliation, once he saw that I am who I am and he couldn't push my buttons—because I don't have many— he lost interest and eventually sat down."[3]

That was the first of many incidents in which Ferguson realized just how isolated he was. But Ferguson is even-tempered and calm. He knows who he is and he is comfortable with that.

He's also absolutely determined "that we're going to get where we want to be."[4]

By November, Ferguson had begun getting there. He had started to build trust among his students, and while many barriers still lay in his path, he was on his way to reaching and teaching these deprived boys. "I thoroughly enjoyed it because you could teach but also because there were so many small people problems every day."[5]

Note that Ferguson has several healthy personality traits, and they all flow from and support each other. He's autonomous—as Maslow would put it, he's "relatively independent from his physical and social environment."[6] He's objective to the point of detachment from the slings and insults. He's laid back and focused outward on the problems and challenges at hand. He's obviously open to experience, empathic to these students, and quite realistic about his circumstances. He's also dutiful, and while he has clear-cut goals in mind, he loved what he was doing on a daily basis. Eight traits are included there; plus, Ferguson is egalitarian. The fact that he enunciated several of these personality characteristics without realizing it, in a matter of seconds—shows how natural and self-reinforcing these virtues are.

Not all those who care and interact with others effectively become leaders of major organizations. But you can see and hear a leader emerging in Ferguson. When he first learned that he'd received one of the coveted teaching posts with Teach for America, Ferguson took it a step further, requesting additional independence and responsibility—in other words, an extra tough assignment. He actually fought for his position at L. W. Beecher Elementary School in New Haven, which was uncharted territory for TFA. Professional as well as personal autonomy are important to Ferguson, who prides himself on his ability to address people problems and come up with solutions, no matter how tough it can be.

"I'm not good if I'm told no," he admits. "I'm also not good if I'm told 'This is the way you've got to do it.' Even as a little kid, I never let my parents dress me . . . I don't work well that way."[7]

At L. W. Beecher, Ferguson got what he wanted—a lot of freedom when it came to developing his curriculum and finding creative ways to really have an impact on the students. He took them to a program called Nature's Classroom, where they had seven hundred acres of forest and farmland to explore. For the first time in their lives, these city kids were shoveling horse manure and holding goats. Ferguson watched with delight as their tough-guy urban demeanor melted away and they became exactly what they were: eleven- and twelve-year-old children.

To teach his students math, he took the whole group to IKEA and gave them a $10,000 imaginary budget. They could furnish their imaginary six-bedroom apartment any way they saw fit, as long as it was under budget. To teach geometry, he had small groups construct a building at least four feet tall. "Fantastic teamwork experience, and all but one of sixteen teams had a building at the end."[8]

At the end of his first year, Ferguson created a book full of pictures of the youngsters and the adventures they'd had, both in and outside the classroom, and printed sixty-eight copies, one for each student. No one had ever gotten a yearbook before, and the self-recognition and affirmation were profound. Ferguson even got the mayor of New Haven to pay a visit to the classroom to hear the children explain their efforts to battle global climate change.

Andrew Ferguson never thought he'd be a teacher. In fact, he'd known since he was four years old that he wanted to get a law degree. But he wanted to do something between college and law school that gave him significant responsibility and independence—and something that could have an impact on a big scale. Teach for America offered the perfect opportunity to do so.

But why would a talented college graduate destined for a law degree choose to teach disadvantaged kids in a run-down trailer for two long years? For Ferguson, it's a matter of fairness. "Any sport you look at, everyone plays by the same rules," he explained. "Who wins is dependent upon how well you work as a team, your skill, and how many hours you practice. Take that analogy to life. Sure, you have the same rules, but it's like one kid's trying to play basketball wearing a fifty-pound weight on his back."[9]

When asked why he cares about the kid carrying the extra fifty-pound weight, Ferguson replied, "Because I didn't have one."[10]

Ferguson was born in a relatively affluent suburb of Pittsburgh and grew up in a good, nurturing family that encouraged him to learn, face challenges, and be creative in finding solutions. Just a zip code away, children in inner-city Pittsburgh faced quite a different reality. "So much has been given to me, and I consider myself lucky for so many reasons. Because of where I was born, and because of the parents to whom I was born, I've had so many opportunities. With these kids, it doesn't matter how hard they've worked. Just trace where they were born. Because these kids were born in a different area, they're not going to get the same shot."[11] Ferguson feels that we all deserve our shot and that he's no better than anyone else. He may be more capable than some, but that's not the same as better.

Ferguson's role models include Bill and Melinda Gates, whose private foundation addresses big issues with millions, even billions, of their dollars. "What they're doing is a really good example of a concerted, driven effort to address problems in a really smart way."[12] Another hero is Bill Strickland, the CEO and founder of Manchester Craftsmen's Guild in Pittsburgh. The guild is a nonprofit, multidiscipline learning community that offers educational classes and arts programs in one of the roughest neighborhoods in Pittsburgh. The Guild has become a model for community organizations nationwide.

"Bill created this huge, fantastic environment with arts and music," Ferguson said. "A whole diverse group of folks come there—from high school kids getting off the bus to adults in the community getting out of jail."[13]

Inside his small, dilapidated classroom, Andrew Ferguson took significant strides in the same direction. Not only did he complete his two-year commitment to Teach for America, he stayed with the New Haven school district for a third, highly rewarding year. Today he is in law school, and he hopes to use his law degree to find systematic ways to address the larger societal issues he saw up close as a teacher.

"I'm still in touch with all these kids. As much as they enjoyed it, I probably enjoyed it ten times more."[14]

As he drives through downtown Pittsburgh each morning on the way to the University of Pittsburgh Law School, Ferguson has time to reflect on crafting a life that suits him. "It's the same time when all the folks are parking their cars and walking into their buildings. I stop at a stoplight and look at their faces. If you were to look at my face when I went into L. W. Beecher, it was not their face. I want to be certain that whatever I do, I'm always excited and I never look like them."[15]

At twenty-six, Andrew Ferguson is the youngest of the great human beings I've interviewed. But he understands better than anyone that age doesn't matter, nor does your race, your religion, where or how you were raised, your sex or sexuality, or your social standing. What matters is your character, your behavior, and whether you're open to learning and improving your lot in life. Ferguson is a true egalitarian soul—someone who believes in the inherent equality of all human beings. In this chapter, we'll learn how people with what Maslow called a "democratic character structure" view others and themselves.

Maslow's Take

The people Maslow calls "self-actualizing" are individuals, he wrote, that are "democratic people in the deepest possible sense . . . They can be and are friendly with anyone of suitable character regardless of class, education, political belief, race, or color. As a matter of fact it often seems as if they are not even aware of these differences, which are for the average person so obvious and important."[16]

The psychologically strong see through the superficial trappings of each person to the being within—or, as Maslow puts it, it's almost as if they don't see those trappings at all. They are largely unconcerned with hierarchy, with issues of race, gender, age, ethnicity, or social standing. For profoundly healthy people, the introductory words of the Declaration of Independence are more than just an idea; they *do* treat everyone as if we've all been created equal, because in their minds, we have been. Maslow wrote, "Most profound, but also most vague is the hard-to-get-at tendency to give a certain quantum of respect to *any* human being just because he or she is a human individual; our subjects seem not to wish to go beyond a certain minimum point, even with scoundrels, of demeaning, or derogating, or robbing of dignity."[17]

Because these people are inwardly satisfied, they are also outwardly focused. Responsibility comes naturally to them. Like Andrew Ferguson, they actually push for it. They want to do their part to make the world a better, fairer place—and even, to push William James's great hope, that all human hearts get their chance. People who possess egalitarian souls typically aren't power hungry. While many want and do rise to positions of authority with perks and acclaim, this rise is usually a derivative of their efforts, not a primary goal and certainly not a need. As Andrew Ferguson noted, "If money and power and fame are ultimately the end goals, people tend not to be successful. Something else is missing."[18] That "something else" is the genuine, democratic interest in other human beings and their plight.

Healthy, happy individuals are also far less concerned with their own standing, whether economic, social, or otherwise. It's not only because most often they have achieved an elevated status, it's because they simply put less value in it. They also don't measure their self-worth by how the world measures it. And when someone challenges them—like the boy who stood up and yelled obscenities in Ferguson's classroom—they remain unruffled. They're comfortable with who they are (chapter 1), and with that self-knowledge comes a serenity (chapter 9) that serves them well in all their pursuits.

John Paul Stevens, "Judge" of the Supreme Court

In the April 11, 2010, *New York Times,* Jeffrey L. Fisher, associate professor at Stanford Law School and Supreme Court clerk from 1998 to 1999, recounted an incident in the U.S. Supreme Court when Chief Justice William Rehnquist was focused on titles and hierarchy and Justice Paul Stevens was not. One day,

> a lawyer was arguing in the court for the first time. When asked a question by Justice Anthony Kennedy, the nervous lawyer started her response with, "Well, Judge—"
>
> Chief Justice William Rehnquist interrupted her. "That's Justice Kennedy," he said.
>
> Shaken, the lawyer continued. A few minutes later, she responded to Justice David Souter by saying, "Yes, Judge." Chief Justice Rehnquist corrected her again: "That's Justice Souter." A couple of minutes later, she called Chief Justice Rehnquist himself a judge.
>
> The chief justice leaned forward, his deep voice now at its sternest, to say, "Counsel is admonished that this court is made up of justices, not judges."
>
> Before the lawyer could say anything, Justice Stevens interjected: "It's O.K., Counsel. The Constitution makes the same mistake."[19]

Not even a chief justice could argue with that. The lesson here: when puncturing a powerful person's air of superiority, do it indirectly—and preferably with humor.

Lincoln and Douglass—More Egalitarians

During the years of the Civil War, our great nation was writhing in bloody battle and civic unrest because of perceived differences due to race. No one understood that better than President Abraham Lincoln. The first Republican president was fully aware of the racial divisions that were tearing his beloved Union apart. But that didn't stop him from treating everyone as his equal, including African American citizens.

Frederick Douglass, the great black orator, was an early critic of President Lincoln. But after the Emancipation Proclamation, Douglass became an ardent supporter of the president. Even before that, he was extremely impressed with the democratic character of Lincoln's personality.

At a speech he gave in 1863, Douglass told a rapt audience the way he had been welcomed by the president: "I will tell you how he received me—just as you have seen one gentleman receive another; with a hand and a voice well-balanced between a kind cordiality and a respectful reserve. I tell you I felt big there!"[20]

Psychologically healthy individuals don't lump people into groups the way others do. They have a fresher, baggage-free perspective when they meet new people. Not only does this give them a truer view of an individual; it gives them a more egalitarian outlook on all humankind. For Lincoln, Frederick Douglass wasn't "a black man." He was a human being and a leader. Lincoln treated Douglass with a healthy dose of respect. That's something that psychologically strong people do.

In generations past, showing respect wasn't just a sign of a kindly nature; it was good manners. When I studied at St. George's

School in Newport, Rhode Island, the school food was so bad that I would regularly belittle Miss Pierce, an aging mouse of a woman who was the school dietician. One day, Robin Rogers, an esteemed English teacher and my advisor, overheard me and barked, "Van de Mark! Come here." Then, out of earshot of everyone else, he said, "Don't you understand that the measure of a gentleman is not how well he treats his superiors, but how well he treats his subordinates?"

He was a wise man that Robin Rogers. He elevated my sense of self while simultaneously putting me in my place! Years later, I often recall that lesson. One place I'd remember it was the halls of CNN, and specifically the lion's den that was the office of Lou Dobbs.

An Example of Not Being Egalitarian

Of the many mega-achievers I've interviewed, only a few qualify for membership in Maslow's elite group. Plenty of people are very good at what they do, but mainly because they're smart, dogged, and focused. Beyond those traits, they're a mix of strengths and weaknesses, virtues and faults. High-performance people with less-healthy psyches often lack the egalitarian nature that distinguishes the merely successful from the great human being. Often they can be aggressively hierarchical.

Take, for example, Lou Dobbs. Nothing is worse than watching someone use their station in life to make harsh comparisons and even demean those of lower status. At CNN, Lou Dobbs did that a lot. He would skewer people in front of large office gatherings. According to a friend who overheard the following, Lou once forced a small, fearful producer to stand on a chair in his office "So, I can yell at you man-to-man!" Lou is at least six foot three inches tall and well over two hundred pounds.

Luckily, I got along well with Lou. He could be charming and funny. But his nature was fundamentally hierarchical. Once when I was walking by his office, he called me in to shoot the breeze. He wanted the latest newsroom gossip and quizzed me as he paced back and forth behind his desk, smoking. (Smoking was strictly prohibited at CNN by order of Ted Turner himself. But Lou feared no one.)

Out of the blue, Lou turned to me and asked, "Don't you wish you were as smart as me?"

I demurred with "Well . . . I wish I was as powerful as you." "Nah," he looked me straight in the eye, "Don't you wish you were as *smart* as me?"

I hesitated and then replied, "Don't you mean 'as smart as, *I*?'"

Taken aback, Lou asked, "What did I say?"

"As *me*."

Lou looked as if he didn't know whether to thank me or punch me. Mercifully, his phone rang and when he picked it up, I scrambled out the door.

Lou is smart and very intimidating—people are right to be afraid of him. The guy's a former marine. But in my opinion, his highly hierarchical management style didn't make the business division at CNN any better. I think it made it worse. People don't make the best choices when they're bullied.

It's sobering to remember that there are people like Lou Dobbs everywhere. He's no different than a huge proportion of bosses—using fear to motivate.

When I think of great bosses who are more egalitarian in their leadership styles, I think of Charles Schwab, Anita Roddick of the Body Shop, Andy Grove of Intel (who worked out of a cubicle like all the other engineers) or Jack Welch. Welch was tough but he also collapsed the organizational chart at General Electric and encouraged workers to take on their bosses in dramatic debating forums called "Work Outs." Surprisingly, I also think of four-time America's Cup sailing champion Dennis Conner. Conner is a prickly guy who can be combative with the press and others. But he works hard to *not* intimidate his crewmates. At least this is what he told me: "You can go yell and scream at a guy and that might make his performance worse because he's already trying his best and you make him nervous."[21]

Of course, some hierarchies, such as the military's, are necessary. But even within these, healthy human beings tend to treat everyone with respect. They're not fixated on someone's rank because they realize that good organizations are fluid and that each person within the group has his or her own role and perspective. And selfishly, they know that anyone can have information that is critical to them. (See chapter 8 on being realistic and Andy Grove's advice of making yourself available to people throughout an organization who want and need to influence you.)

How You Can Become More Egalitarian

To become more egalitarian, first, recognize the humanity in all of us. Simply understanding that every person has consciousness and thus feelings and wounds makes most of us at least sympathetic if not empathic.

Second, recognize your own ignorance, the vast store of knowledge that the rest of humanity has, and the fact that you can learn from others if you give them some respect.

And third, for all you mercenaries out there, remember that even the lowest-paid functionary can trip you up if slighted. I learned that lesson in the White House when I was starting out as a reporter. I was young and ambitious—a man in a hurry. And men and women in a hurry are often brusque, even short-tempered. One day in 1984, I needed some snippet of information about the timing of an announcement. One of the perky press office assistants got flustered when I pressed her for answers and I was short with her—maybe even derisive. Not long after that, I was left out of an important photo opportunity. I learned my lesson the hard way. But I had to learn it only once.

You never know whom you're going to need. You never know who's going to rise to prominence and power. And furthermore, life itself is moral. You can find much more on the karma of life in chapter 3, where the trait is being ethical. Suffice it to say that your behavior is the standard by which you are judged. It's your currency. The way we treat each other is the ends as well as the means. And difficult, snobbish, or abrasive personalities *ought* to be penalized.

On top of those good reasons, democracy, meritocracy, and the efficiency of a society, let alone an economy, depend on offering opportunities to any and all who wish to pursue them. An economy that's based on meritocracy rather than hierarchy is one of the biggest reasons that the United States remains globally competitive despite our higher labor costs and environmental regulations. Being egalitarian is not just good, it's wise.

Takeaways

No matter how high they rise in society, the good among the great remain naturally egalitarian because of their penetrating appreciation for every human being, regardless of station. They're also humble in a way because they recognize the reality of their own ignorance and know that they can learn something from nearly everyone—indeed, that very often critical information comes up from the lower rungs of every organization.

- ✓ Resist categorizing individuals—by any method.
- ✓ Find commonalities with your rivals and your enemies.
- ✓ Treat everyone with respect—especially your subordinates.
- ✓ Behave as religions teach—that each human spirit or soul is sacred and everlasting.
- ✓ Being smarter or more capable does not make you better. There's much more to being a better human being than being clever and accomplished.
- ✓ Remember that life can be capricious, and thus there's real truth to the old adage "There, but for the grace of God go I."

....

Chapter 12

Laugh with Me

TRAIT: *JOLLY*

Joy in one's heart and some laughter on one's lips is a sign that the person down deep has a pretty good grasp of life.

—HUGH SIDEY

IN THE 1950S, A quiet little boy lived a lonely existence in Bloomfield Hills, Michigan, just outside Detroit. His father was a senior executive at Lincoln-Mercury, his mother a former model. In the big house where they lived, this boy had an entire floor to himself. But he spent most of the time playing in the expansive basement, animating his two thousand toy soldiers with funny voices and sound effects. That boy grew up to be Robin Williams.

As one of the preeminent comedians of our age, Williams has created quite a legacy for himself. Unfortunately, his descent into and recovery from alcoholism and drug abuse in recent years as well as two divorces have tainted that legacy. But beneath the addiction and heartbreak is a very funny, very lovable character. And one reason Williams is lovable as well as comic is that his brand of humor is rarely hostile or caustic. He's zany, irreverent, and lightning quick, not cruel or arrogant.

In his early days as a stand-up comedian, Williams made a name for himself with the manic absurdity of his act. He dazzled audiences with his fast-paced humor and hilarious characterizations. He was a blur of funny faces and voices, buoying his sets with impressions, jokes, ad libs, and boundless energy.

After spending a few years at Juilliard, Williams got his first big break when he was cast as the alien Mork on *Happy Days*, which eventually led to the title role in the well-known spin-off series, *Mork and Mindy*. The show's premise allowed Williams to embrace one of the most prominent features of his particular brand of comedy: childlike wonder. For Mork, the whole world was a weird and wondrous place. This suited Williams just fine, as he got to demonstrate his virtuosic knack for mimicry and downright silliness.

Then came *Good Morning, Vietnam*, a movie that earned Williams his first Oscar nomination. Director Barry Levinson allowed him to ad-lib all of his broadcasts as DJ Adrian Cronauer. The result? Comic gold.

"And now, here are the headlines. Here they come right now. Pope actually found to be Jewish. The East Germans, today, claimed the Berlin Wall was a fraternity prank. Also the Pope decided today to release Vatican-related bath products. An incredible thing, yes, it's the new Pope-on-a-Rope. That's right. Pope-on-a-Rope. Wash with it, go straight to heaven. Thank you."[1]

The genius of Robin Williams lies in the fact that he relishes the absurd, specifically the absurd nature of humankind. He doesn't need to rip others apart because he gets the joke of human beings—we're silly, crazy, unpredictable creatures who have a lot to laugh about. Williams doesn't laugh at any individual's expense because he helps us all laugh at our own expense.

Most, it not all, of the good among the great people I've profiled have a good sense of humor. Many have a great one. But the jokes they tell or laugh at aren't the same ones that appeal to the big audiences filled with the lowest common denominator. Their humor is of a more philosophical bent. Much like parables, their jokes often contain double or parallel meanings that puncture the self-importance of the mighty and teach us about ourselves.

In this chapter, we'll look at the exceptional humor of exceptional human beings and maybe even have a few laughs along the way.

Maslow's Take

According to Maslow, self-actualizing people "do not consider funny what the average person considers to be funny. Thus, they do not laugh at hostile humor (making people laugh by hurting someone) or superiority humor (laughing at someone else's inferiority) or authority-rebellion humor (the unfunny, Oedipal, or smutty joke)."[2]

In other words, exceptional individuals prefer a philosophical rather than a barbed or self-absorbed type of humor. They're more aware of the absurdity of humankind. Is it any wonder the best comedians are self-deprecating? Their jokes are generally less hierarchical and less sarcastic than those of their colleagues and more genuinely funny as a result.

Healthy, happy people laugh easily, and they laugh for the right reasons: at silliness and tension relievers, at harmless slapstick and everyday absurdities. Think of Lucille Ball. You can't even imagine her slinging insults. Most of all, the best laugh *at* themselves and *with* others. They don't take themselves or their status too seriously. Their humor is not cynical or demeaning. And very often they laugh at their troubles, their aches and pains. As Poosie Orr (chapter 2) put it, "You've got to! Particularly when you get older."[3]

When you see those who care about and interact with others effectively interviewed, they're more likable; they say things that help the rest of us relax because they acknowledge their own foibles and shortcomings. We see and identify with their humanity and we're thrilled to have anything in common.

Unhappy people aren't the only ones who tend to laugh at insults and sarcasm. Unfortunately, most people like hostile humor, and usually, the meaner the funnier. We all celebrate rapier wits and tart-tongued critics. Television hits such as *Will and Grace* and *The Fresh Prince of Bel-Air* were built on characters who communicate through put-downs.

Another example is Joan Rivers, whose comic style was full of insults. For a time, she made a career out of her well-aimed barbs: Barbra Streisand nose jokes, Elizabeth Taylor fat jokes, and so on. Then she shifted and plumbed self-deprecation and tension relievers. She developed a set of gags that humanized her, making her likable to a wider audience. Also, I used to know Joan—I even spent Christmas week with her in 1999—and her caustic edge is mostly an act. These days her humor can still bite. But she's at her best when she's more philosophical.

Among the superhealthy historic figures whom Maslow cites is Abraham Lincoln, who Maslow felt had the most nonhostile humor, which Maslow also calls "existential" or "self-actualizing." In Doris Kearns Goodwin's wonderful biography of Lincoln and his top cabinet officers, *Team of Rivals,* she cites Lincoln's humor fifteen times, and not once is it caustic or cruel. Even when he had come down with a mild case of smallpox, the great liberator had a joke to tell. "Yes it is a bad disease, but it has its advantages. For the first time I have something now to give everybody that calls!"[4]

Using wit to disarm others rather than attack them is a favorite method of a breakthrough contemporary comic named Ellen.

Self-Deprecating Style

When Ellen DeGeneres started doing stand-up comedy in New Orleans in the 1980s, she was known for her whimsical, quirky routine. Her most famous line began "My grandmother started walking five miles a day when she was sixty. She's ninety-seven today. We don't know where the hell she is."

Over the last thirty years, DeGeneres has made quite a name for herself—and not just because she's gay. Her kooky sense of humor and deadpan delivery drew comparisons to Bob Newhart, and in the 1980s, she was named the funniest person in America after winning a Showtime competition. In the mid-'90s, she amassed an even wider following with her own sitcom, *Ellen*.

Yet despite her superstar status, she's incredibly down-to-earth. Her genial, "just another girl" comedic style nets her a whole lot of laughs. She excels at conversational humor, which is why she's such a great talk show host (and she's got the Emmys to prove it). No one is better than Ellen at taking simple lines and delivering them with perfect timing for optimal punch. "Everybody wants the best jack-o-lantern ever . . . A lot of people get them at the grocery store or a pumpkin patch, and that is expensive and hard. So do what I do kids—steal a pumpkin."[5]

DeGeneres's willingness to get a laugh at her own expense is another way she endears herself to audiences worldwide. She never makes any pretense of artificial superiority in her comedy. In fact, some of her best humor comes from mining her own experiences.

"I didn't know what I wanted to do," she told the Class of '09 at Tulane University. "I shucked oysters, I was a hostess, I was a bartender, I was a waitress, I painted houses, I sold vacuum cleaners, I had no idea. And I thought I'd just finally settle in some job, and I would make enough money to pay my rent—maybe have basic cable, maybe not. I didn't really have a plan.

"My point is that, by the time I was your age, I really thought I knew who I was, but I had no idea. Like for example, when I was your age, I was dating men. So what I'm saying is, when you're older, most of you will be gay."[6]

How You Can Become More Jolly

It's not easy to abandon put-downs and zingers. First of all, television comedies are often built on them. Currently, NBC's *30 Rock* is wickedly funny, but nearly all of the gags are jabs. In fact, in one episode, Liz Lemon attends her high school reunion and is loathed by her classmates because of her tart tongue. One of my best friends watches in wonder—not because the show is so funny (and it is!) but because the zingers are so fast, furious, and personal. He prefers *Seinfeld*, where Jerry, Kramer, George, and Elaine are hilarious as they reveal the absurdity of everyday life and just make it through the day.

Second, for many of us, being caustically critical is all the humor we've got. When she was interviewed for a public television series I wrote called *Great Entrepreneurs*, Martha Stewart confessed, "After my divorce, I realized that being too critical was one of the reasons. So, I stopped being so critical . . . and I lost 30 percent of my personality!"[7]

Dropping your caustic comments may cost you part of your personality, at least until you develop other sources and senses of humor. Nevertheless, if Stewart can learn to be less critical, so can you.

Having this kind of sense of humor is one of Maslow's more subtle traits, so, if you're unconvinced that hostile humor is really a bad thing, then remember that cruelty very often starts with it. Think back to your schoolyard days, when picking on someone who was weaker or different started with teasing, mockery, and poking fun. Even the language of bullying is often about humor. And bullies use put-downs as a way of masking their cruel intent. Somehow, if you're laughing at someone you have license to also hurt that person. It's a way of cutting someone out of the herd, making them separate and thus vulnerable to attack.

So, if you want to change the way you amuse yourself as well as others, begin by turning some of the critical spotlight back on yourself. Not only will you feel how harsh it can be, but you'll be able to laugh at your own shortcomings and let others laugh with you. It's a good way to get some perspective on your humor as well as yourself.

I've had plenty of firsthand experience with hostile humor. As a boy, I turned my rivals' quirks and weaknesses into schoolyard jokes and I got a lot of laughs. It was self-defense, but it was often mean and costly. Little did I realize that the cost was to me as well as my targets. Sometimes I did it to deflect the attention of bullies, even to win their respect. I felt I was justified because I was often the object of derision, but the more I did it, the more resentment I sowed in others.

Until one day when I was twelve or thirteen, I got into a scuffle with Thane Woodside, one of my pals. And there, scrapping on the ground, I realized the cost of my poisonous tongue. All the boys huddled over us were rooting for Thane. Thane was a good guy, but so was I, I thought. I was shocked and demoralized at the hostility from boys I thought were friends. It drained my energy. I lost the fight and I've never forgotten it.

If you find yourself laughing at other people's expense, spend some time studying the humor of those who get laughs without attacking others. Robin Williams and Ellen DeGeneres are two great comedians to watch. Notice how they love puns, plays on words, irony, and absurdity. Even bathroom humor, though admittedly childish and vulgar, is usually harmless.

Fine-tune your observational skills (which will make you more wedded to reality, chapter 8) to identify personality quirks and funny truths about the way people operate. In 2006, DeGeneres told *Redbook*, "I just like observing people—it's something I've done ever since I was a kid, and I got really good at it. That's a big part of why I became a comedian. My audience is filled with every kind of person you can imagine, and I love that."[8] DeGeneres's humor is born of understanding and empathy (more on that in the next chapter). No wonder she doesn't tear people down. Instead, this out-of-the-closet lesbian relates to them, which is what makes her likable and gives her the ability to break through the fear of and prejudice against people who are attracted to the same sex.

The better you become at observing others, the more you'll appreciate the wacky ways in which we behave, see ourselves, and create our endless predicaments. These are great sources of a more philosophical amusement, which is fitting. Maslow writes that the best among us "are ordinarily concerned with basic issues and eternal questions of the type we have learned to call philosophical or ethical."[9] And this juxtaposition of the mundane and the eternal is the source of so much humor and self-recognition at the same time.

This is different than finding something painful or embarrassing in someone else and then exploiting it for laughs. Instead, it's seeing the humor in real-life situations of which we are all a part. Or even more astutely, finding humor in universal pain. Even in the darkest days of the U.S. Civil War, Abraham Lincoln could find an amusing anecdote to tell. Once, at a dinner given by Secretary of State Henry Seward, Lincoln told a "tale about young women during the War of 1812 who made belts with engraved mottoes to give their lovers departing for battle. When one young girl suggested 'Liberty or Death!' her soldier protested that the phrase was 'rather strong.' Couldn't she make it 'Liberty or Be Crippled' instead?"[10] Healthy, happy human beings know that humor is everywhere and that they don't have to be snarky or nasty to make it that way.

So remember, we're not laughing *at* you; we're laughing *toward* you—and ourselves!

Takeaways

Having what Abraham Maslow calls a "nonhostile sense of humor" is one of the more subtle traits of the good among the great. But once you examine the basis of so much of today's comedy, you see the embedded cruelty. And if you get better at observing and absorbing the absurdities of human behavior, you'll find an endless source of more absurd, more philosophical amusement.

- ✓ Recall your daily intentions versus what actually happened to you to see how our life veers from the mundane to the absurd.
- ✓ Laugh at your aches and pains. The alternative is intolerable.
- ✓ Think of random setbacks as "cosmic jokes."
- ✓ Remember that many of the world's religions have among their gods the trickster god.
- ✓ Observe (and enjoy) comedians who get laughs without being hostile, aggressive, superior, or smutty.
- ✓ Never make jokes at other people's expense.
- ✓ Hone your observational skills to find the quirky, silly, and absurd in others' behavior.
- ✓ Make the following your motto: "We're not laughing *at* you; we're laughing *toward* you!"

Chapter 13

....

It's Not about You

TRAIT: *EMPATHIC*

The great gift of human beings is that we have the power of empathy. We can all sense a mysterious connection to each other.

—MERYL STREEP

EMPATHY CAN MAKE YOU rich. Don't believe me? Believe Charles Schwab.

In the spring of 2010, Schwab, founder and CEO of the Charles Schwab Corporation, had a fortune of approximately $4.7 billion and was listed in the Forbes 400 as the fiftieth richest man in the United States. In 2009, Schwab's firm had $1.2 trillion (yes, trillion!) under management.[1]

Schwab launched the discount brokerage powerhouse that bears his name simply because he "felt that the financial service business had developed a brokerage industry that wasn't empathetic toward customers; they were empathetic toward themselves."[2]

We all know that empathy gives us greater sensitivity toward other human beings. We may also figure out that being empathic can win you friends and allies. What we may not know is that the ability to identify with others' wants and needs, hopes and fears can translate into spectacular success because when people get beyond their own neediness, they're able to see the world from a limitless number of perspectives. Talk about being an astute observer! Empathizing makes the good among the great highly sensitive, multiocular visionaries.

Those who empathize with others not only see more, but see specific situations in a clearer and more nuanced way because they react as a variety of people would. These added insights give them a huge advantage when it comes to *anticipating* others' wants, needs, and opinions. (Better reality recognition—chapter 8—and empathy both help you anticipate the future.) Schwab is not the first financial titan to recognize the value of anticipation to get to the top. When asked what his secret to success was as head of Merrill Lynch in the 1970s, Donald Regan, who was secretary of the treasury and White House chief of staff under Ronald Reagan, said, "That's not a big conversation. It's one word—anticipation."[3]

Schwab's particular brand of empathy is powerful because it springs from one of humankind's fundamental positive drivers: fairness or justice. "I don't know what it was that got me to the point of thinking this way," Schwab told me, "but I felt it was about *fairness* . . . a sense of values. A sense that there is a human behind every business, and the more human you are, the more you can relate to your customer. And the more you relate to your customer, the more you are going to create new services and relationships that will enhance your organization."[4]

When I pressed him on the origins of his approach, Schwab responded like most great leaders who are also good people, by stating first that he hadn't thought about it much. "You know, you don't do a lot of that kind of self-analysis. But I went to a very religious educational process in grades one to six, and I had these incredible nuns that just banged on me all the time about these kinds of things called values. And, I'm not an overly religious person today and haven't been, but I think that early training did me a lot of good."[5]

I interjected that of course he was going to get a lot of debate over whose values or what values ought to be taught.

"You know," he responded, "when you study about religion and philosophy and things like that, there's such a common theme among all of the world religions, that it probably doesn't make any difference."

"All of them stand for honesty and treating your fellow person well?"

"There are other people in your life other than yourself. You're not doing things in life just for your own self-satisfaction. You are doing things because you have relationships around you and you've got to serve your family, then your larger community . . . as you go up the channel."[6] (Note here that Schwab's empathy now morphs into a sense of duty to others. We'll discuss great individuals' self-imposed duty to a wider community in chapter 14.)

When I asked if he derives "psychic benefits" from running his business with this mind-set, Schwab who is typically quite contained, replied enthusiastically, "I do! I have felt that this company is a very fair company. To this day, twenty-six or twenty-seven years later, I think you will travel throughout the country and go into any Schwab office, and the employees will tell you that this is a fair company. 'They treat me fairly, we treat our customers fairly.' That's a pretty nice thing to be proud about, and I'm very proud about it."[7]

Schwab's empathy for the small investor led him to push for deregulation and then stiff competition to drive down brokerage commissions. He was also the first to offer twenty-four-hour telephone access and the first to offer on-line trading, as well as mutual funds other than his own. And in late 2009, he launched four ETFs (exchange traded funds) charging no brokerage fees.

"My vision happens to be that every American is an investor for their long-term assets—their retirement assets," Schwab said. "They'll get better returns. They'll have better incomes. They'll have more choices when they get older. They'll have more choices while they are going through their life cycle, whether it's choices for the kids through education, choices for a second home or first home— whatever it might be. It is all about having financial wherewithal to have these choices as we go through life's wonderful opportunities."[8]

Schwab's empathy has given him more than a strong moral compass and prescience about investor needs. It has given him genuine warmth and trustworthiness, which has made him one of the most trusted pitchmen in the history of advertising. His "Q" rating—a marketer's survey of a media figure's likability and trustworthiness—is sky high. Most CEOs, even most company founders, flop when they become pitchmen.

Like all the good among the great, Schwab is forthcoming about his philosophy, both where he got it and why it's been critical to his success. When I asked if he realized that building a business based on fairness, of all things, was risky, he replied, "It must have been a risk. In some respects, I am sure some of my closest friends thought I was probably the most naïve person in the world. And that is probably the benefit of youth—you don't know how naïve you really are at the time. All you have is passion about whatever it is that are your values. And I had deep passions. I have pretty deep passions about the same things to this day."⁹

Why is it that many successful people like Charles Schwab, entrepreneurs in particular, feel such a strong connection to other people in the world? According to Schwab, "I think any business is essentially about relationships. Whatever the enterprise, whether it's financial services or selling widgets of some kind, the way you develop your customer base, your consumer base, is having important and in-depth relationships. At Schwab we try to be 'continuing.' It's unrelenting what we go through here in trying to determine the next level of relationship. How can we do it better? How can we make it more polished? If this is not working, how we can scrap that and create a new version of what it is?"¹⁰

So many people are interested in achieving material wealth, but they get it backwards—they go after the money instead of going after the relationship. What Schwab is saying is that money is really a by-product of success, not the goal itself.

> I can remember having my first conversation with our early set of employees, when there were only about fifteen or twenty of us. And I kept saying, back in 1975 or 1976, "What do we want to become as a company?" I kept using the phrase that I wanted to be the best at what we did at that time and the best at what we are going to do five years from the day and ten years from the day. I didn't want to be the biggest.
>
> There would be a by-product though; if we really are the best, we become the biggest. And we become the most profitable. But a business really starts from the customer relationship. You create revenue from the customer somehow. They pay you for services. And if you are a really great company, you go through all these different expenses, and at the end of

the day, there may be something called the "bottom line" and what we call "profit." Hopefully a great company will have profit. A not-so-good company won't.[11]

In 2009, the Charles Schwab Corporation had net profits of $205 million.

In this chapter, we're going to see how the trait of empathy is imperative to our development as psychologically mature individuals. If you want to move toward the kind of groundbreaking success Charles Schwab has experienced, start identifying with other human beings every chance you get.

Maslow's Take

Schwab talks a lot about serving families and communities, both in his business and in his personal life. It's fitting that he's also a good family person because most, if not all, great individuals see themselves as deeply enveloped within their families as well as within their communities and the larger family of humankind. Abraham Maslow wrote that these individuals "love or rather have compassion for all humanity."[12]

In *Motivation and Personality*, Maslow writes that "Self-actualizing people have a deep feeling of identification, sympathy, and affection for human beings in general. They feel kinship and connection, as if all people were members of a single family." Because of this, they "have a genuine desire to help the human race."[13] Note that they don't agree or identify with the foolish, unethical, and shortsighted behavior of most of us. Maslow wrote that the best "are often saddened, exasperated, and even enraged by the shortcomings of the average person."[14]

Maslow makes a strong point that people with healthy psyches who are empathic identify with others beyond their own communities, cultures, and often even beyond those who are alive when they are. Just as their egalitarian outlook allows them to see beyond superficial differences, they can relate to people no matter their age, level of education, standing, or skin color. I've found that many even have empathy for animals and nature overall. They are focused on others, problem solving, and the greater good, in the widest frame of reference.

Abraham Lincoln's Empathy and Humility

Empathizing with people we know and love—our friends, family, and peers—is easy. But why do exceptional human beings show uncommon empathy for people whom, by all accounts, they could regard with condescension or simply disregard?

In a word, the reason is *humility*. Maslow writes that the best among us "are all quite well aware of how little they know in comparison with what *could* be known and what *is* known by others."[15] So even the most successful good people, by any number of measures, will have a realistic and therefore relatively humble assessment of their own knowledge, even when they know much more than everyone around them. The critical reason is that they are both more appreciative of individual differences and less judgmental about them. Add to that their deep-seated self-acceptance and they have few instances to judge themselves harshly.

The result: they don't often judge others harshly, even criminals. Maslow also writes, "Most profound, but also most vague, is the hard-to-get-at tendency to give a certain quantum of respect to any human being just because he or she is a human individual."[16]

Most of us do not see the fundamental humanity in our enemies. Indeed, we demonize them. But the best human beings see commonalities in their foes. A few magnanimous historical figures empathized with their failed competitors and even with their betrayers. Abraham Lincoln was one of them.

Lincoln demonstrated time and time again "a singular ability to transcend personal vendetta, humiliation, or bitterness."[17]

Emulating Lincoln's magnanimous empathy is not easy. The key to developing the same open-mindedness in ourselves is to start small. If people make you angry, instead of immediately spouting off, put yourself in their shoes. Why are they behaving the way they are? What do they want or need that they may not be getting? By taking a moment to step back and assess the situation with coolness and clarity, you'll attain a greater understanding of what's really going on and better control over your reactions.

Empathy is a trait that can take a lifetime to master. Just remember that the first trait in this book, autonomy, has a big dose of acceptance in it—meaning that great and good people accept not only their own faults and foibles but those of humanity in general. They see beyond their own communities and countries and some, notably the artists and scientists, even see and empathize with those other than the human species. Now, in the twenty-first century, there are plenty of people who think globally when it comes to conservation, political cooperation, and spiritual harmony. But this kind of universal empathy is not new. One great, native American example comes to us from Chief Seattle.

Chief Seattle's Empathy for Every Living Thing

In the 1850s, the American government began making "treaties" with the native tribes of the Pacific Northwest. In reality, there wasn't much of a negotiation—the Native Americans were forced to give away their land to the advancing settlers. In return, the government designated relatively small reservations for them to live on, and the tribes received promises of future aid.

In 1854, Chief Seattle, leader of the Suquamish and Duwamish tribes in what is now Washington State, met with U.S. government representatives on a sandy beach. There he is said to have made an impassioned speech in his native tongue. A translator-poet jotted down notes and reconstructed the speech some thirty-three years later in 1887, creating the only eyewitness account of the chief's words (though it probably departed significantly from the original version). Nearly a century later, in 1977, screenwriter Ted Perry used Chief Seattle's speech as a model for the script of a film on ecology called *Home*. This is the version that endures today, one that is soaked in humility and awash in recognition of every living thing. This long dead man of the wilderness summed up his creed this way:

> The earth does not belong to man,
> Man belongs to the earth.
> Man did not weave the web of life,
> He is merely a strand in it.[18]

How You Can Be More Empathic

You can manifest Chief Seattle's humility by putting yourself under a higher authority. The good among the great do this. They are strong and capable and calm when they need to be. They could run roughshod over most people in their path, but they don't. They play fair. They respect others as well as their own elevated ethics. They answer to something higher than themselves. They avoid the great Christian sin of pride in oneself. To a certain degree, the good among the great business leaders see themselves as being in service to their customers, their boards of directors, and even their colleagues and employees. Of course, each has his or her own individual reasons for working as hard and as humbly as he or she does. All I know is that doing so serves each and every one of them well—their sense of service helps them achieve their goals, and they know it.

It certainly makes their successes long lived. It certainly makes their achievements broad as well as deep. Perhaps most of all, it keeps them within a respecting, even loving, network of supporters.

Human beings are incredibly social creatures. It never fails to amaze me that when I walk on Long Island's ninety-mile beach, I see that most people will plop down within a few feet of someone else. Most people also choose to live in cities. We rely on each other. Those of us who choose to live in the countryside know this all too well. We are grateful for good neighbors. We know how tough it can be if the electricity goes out or a twenty-pound raccoon won't leave your kitchen. The good among the great know how tough life is and how important we are to each other. So despite their great talents and insight, they humble themselves before humankind—and their gods.

It's also good to remember that the world today has become a smaller, dirtier, more dangerous place and that our differences grow pale compared to our common motivations, interests, and instincts. So, Chief Seattle is more right than ever. All things are connected.

Surround yourself with people who genuinely care about others. And don't stop there. In your own life, take strides large and small to be someone who thinks of others, who thinks as others do. It will not only win you friends and allies, but broaden your understanding of the world and maybe even help you see the next great business opportunity.

Just ask Charles Schwab.

Takeaways

The gist about empathy is that it's not just about charitable thinking. Indeed, those who consistently put themselves in others' shoes enjoy great advantages in terms of anticipating wants and needs. And they make themselves trusted.

- ✓ When you empathize you see the world from a limitless number of perspectives—giving you greater knowledge and understanding.
- ✓ Empathy is the first step toward anticipating others' needs and wants—invaluable in business and all aspects of service to others.
- ✓ Being sensitive to others is not a sign of weakness but a sign of awareness, which is a strength.
- ✓ Turn conversations toward others' wants, problems, and goals so that you may help them and earn their allegiance.
- ✓ Solving others' problems puts you in a leadership role.
- ✓ Find commonalities with all human beings, even your rivals and enemies. Doing so will give you greater understanding and humble you.

Chapter 14

....

Be Proactive

TRAIT: *DUTIFUL*

*A hero is someone who has given his or her life
to something bigger than oneself.*

—JOSEPH CAMPBELL

IN DECEMBER OF 1956, Andy Grove, the cofounder
of Intel, was twenty years old. But he wasn't Andy Grove then—
his name was still Andres Grof. And he wasn't going to sock hops
or drag races like his peers in America. Far from it: He was flee-
ing his hometown of Budapest, Hungary, to escape an advancing
Red Army from the Soviet Union. If caught, he would have spent
years in a Siberian concentration camp.

"There were four of us" Grove remembered, "We made an
arrangement with a guy who lived near the border and made his
living smuggling goods back and forth. He took us part of the

way, and then he pointed out a bunch of lights on the horizon and said, 'That's Austria, so keep your eyes on it and just go.'

"So we stumbled in plowed fields through the night toward those lights. Every once in a while a flare was shot up in the air and we plopped onto the field so that we would not be seen."[1] The flares were from the border guards, who were positioned on the Austrian border.

"So, we get to one of those lights and we kind of get down on the ground and get a little closer and dogs are barking, and a guy comes out with a lantern and says in Hungarian, 'Who's there?'"[2]

Grove was afraid they had drifted back into Hungary, but the man said, "Come on in. You are in Austria. You are safe."[3]

Andy Grove's escape made him familiar with the cold dread that sours your stomach, muddles your thinking, and skews your choices. It also taught him how to lead despite inadequate information, by proactively probing the unknown in front of him. A skill he employed brilliantly as he guided Intel, the computer chip giant.

"When your business environment changes and your business structure changes and your business model changes, there won't be facts for a while. You have to build up those facts by doing business experiments, starting new businesses—new introductions, new products, new markets—and moving down along the hypothetical paths to gather data. And then refine your strategy. Refine your approach based on the data that you acquire. But, after a period of time, there is no data because everything is new . . . and the Internet is a perfect example of it."[4]

When little or no data is available and when the risks ahead seem particularly large, leaders must also appear more confident than they feel. Why? "Because you have to lead people into uncertainty. And the only thing that you have to lead them with is your own convictions and your own credibility. To have people led, you sometimes have to act more confident than you really are . . .

To act more confident than you really are is not a normal way of operating," Grove explained. "But when you are kind of lost, the leader has to take certain personal risks."[5]

When I asked if that was the same as faking it, Grove shook his head.

"Structure it beyond what you feel comfortable with. 'Faking it' is too strong. You really have to believe in the direction; otherwise, you won't be able to lead people in that way. But you may have to act more decisive than you really feel."[6]

Acting decisively often entails taking big risks, which Grove doesn't deny. What he points out though is that too often people don't properly weigh the risk of inaction, "There's a risk associated with taking action," he says, "and people are very mindful of that. But for every action that has a risk associated with it, there's a countervailing risk associated with *not* taking the action. And very often, people look at the risk associated with the action and don't consider that the default of not taking action may be an even higher risk."[7]

Grove is well-acquainted with risk, responsibility, and duty. Twelve years before he escaped from Hungary, the Nazis deported his father to a slave labor camp. Eight-year-old Andres and his mother were left to fend for themselves. His mother carefully weighed the risks. All they knew and trusted was nearby—in their home, their neighborhood. But she also understood that the risk of inaction—staying put at a time when Jews were being rounded up—was greater than leaving everything behind, including their identities.

"I had to learn to accept, articulate, and act out false identity," Grove said. "I had to memorize my new name on a train ride from where we left our home to where we were going. And I remember sitting on the train and looking out the window and repeating my new name—which was kind of a difficult name—over and over and over and over so I firmed it in my memory. I knew what the stakes were."[8] Even as a little boy, Grove understood that if he forgot this new name, it could not only cost him his life, but cost his mother hers.

When asked if his experience as a child affected the way he managed his business, Grove admitted, "I have no idea. But your personality, your thinking processes, your convictions are all a result of your genes and the environment you grew up in."[9]

Grove is a walking testament to the way our childhood experiences shape our beliefs, our behavior, and our sense of duty. But his story is a reminder that we can escape—not only bigots and armies but our pasts and our outdated thinking. Grove has always looked forward, able to shoulder enormous personal as well as institutional responsibility when his own analysis led him to believe he could see the best way forward.

For example, by 1985 Intel was losing ground to the Japanese in the memory chip business. Sensing an imminent seismic shift, Grove bet the company on more complex microprocessors, the brain for a product that barely existed and certainly one that most people never dreamed would be commonplace: the personal computer.

We all know how that risk played out—in stupendous sales growth for Intel and global domination of a business that supplies the brains to computers. In the years since, Grove has faced even more than corporate business risk, religious persecution, and political oppressors. He has survived a personal battle with prostate cancer. He approached this latest challenge in typical Grove fashion, taking a sabbatical and using an engineer's methodology to assess his condition—or in his terminology, to "study the data." Then, with his doctors, he crafted his own successful treatment.

You may never face cancer, Nazis, or the Red Army. But you can benefit from the techniques that Grove employs: being problem focused, taking responsibility, analyzing data, gathering more data if necessary, testing your convictions, acting with more confidence than you may feel, and recognizing that inaction is often riskier than action. In this chapter, we'll see how.

Maslow's Take

Abraham Maslow reasons that a healthy sense of self-worth makes a person less self-focused, more problem focused, and ultimately willing to take more initiative and carry more responsibility for the greater good, in other words, be dutiful.

He finds that self-actualizing individuals "customarily have some mission in life, some task to fulfill, some problem outside themselves which enlists much of their energies. This is not necessarily a task that they would prefer or choose for themselves; it may be a task that they feel is their responsibility, duty or obligation . . . In general, these tasks are nonpersonal or unselfish, concerned rather with the good of humanity in general or of a nation in general, or of a few individuals in the subject's family."[10]

Why do the good among the great feel such strong obligations to help others? They certainly don't have to take on the duties that they do. No one is forcing them to sacrifice their time, energy, and money. They do it because, as we learned in the last chapter, they also empathize. They feel a kinship with all people. They feel that they have a duty and responsibility to help people who are less fortunate than they are. They are strong and self-sufficient, so in general, they need not focus on their own issues. Instead, the best among us "have a genuine desire to help the human race," according to Maslow.[11] Sometimes that help seems heaven sent, as it did one day on a harrowing flight over New York City.

Captain Sullenberger's Duty

On January 15, 2009, a plane was headed for a crash-landing into the Hudson River. But for the first time in forty-five years, a major aircraft crash-landed in the water without causing a single fatality. Every one of the 155 people on board survived. Captain Chesley B. Sullenberger III—or "Sully," as he is affectionately known—is the man responsible for saving their lives.

US Airways Flight 1549 was headed from New York City to Charlotte, but it didn't get far. Shortly after takeoff, Sullenberger reported to air traffic control that the plane had hit a large flock of birds. This isn't unheard of for commercial airlines—birds will sometimes disable one of the plane's engines. But that day, the birds (presumably a flock of Canada geese) took out *both* engines. "To have zero thrust coming out of those engines was shocking," Sullenberger said in an interview with the Associated Press. "Then silence."[12]

The precrash audiotapes, released by the Federal Aviation Administration, feature an incredibly calm and collected Captain Sullenberger discussing options with air traffic control. At first Sullenberger thinks it may be possible to either return to LaGuardia Airport or land at Teterboro Airport in New Jersey. But then, as the plane rapidly loses altitude, he is forced to make a fast and vital decision. "We're going to be in the Hudson," he says.

After telling the passengers to brace for impact, he made a smooth, flat landing on the river at about 3:30 p.m. Fortunately, they were near a ferry crossing, so aid was almost instantaneous. All of the passengers were safely evacuated as the water level rose. Captain Sullenberger walked the jet's aisle twice to make sure no passengers remained on board. He was the last to exit the plane.

In the days before he became a national hero—long before he received medals of valor and a personal invitation to Barack Obama's presidential inauguration—Sullenberger was a U.S. Air Force fighter pilot flying for his country. He also served as a safety chairman for the Air Line Pilots Association, as well as an accident investigator. You might say assessing risk, handling danger—indeed, protecting others—was his calling. And in January 2009, Sullenberger was called.

"One way of looking at this," he told CBS news anchor Katie Couric, "might be that, for forty-two years, I've been making small, regular deposits in this bank of experience: education and training. And on January 15 the balance was sufficient so that I could make a very large withdrawal."[13]

Note the humility—Sullenberger offloads credit to "experience." The good among the great always deflect credit to others or to luck or to larger forces, if they discuss their successes at all. In fact, Sullenberger's friends describe him as shy and reticent. And like Mary and Melinda Cunningham from chapters 6 and 9, he's also the epitome of grace under pressure. New York City mayor Michael Bloomberg dubbed him "Captain Cool." A colleague at UC Berkeley, where Sullenberger is a visiting professor, said, "I can imagine him being sufficiently in charge to get those people out. He's got that kind of personality, which is to his credit."[14]

Time Magazine named Sullenberger among the 25 "people who mattered" in 2009, along with President Barack Obama and Supreme Court Justice Sonya Sotomayor. The same year, his memoir, *Highest Duty*, was published by HarperCollins.

The notion of duty—obligation or responsibility to something more than yourself—is what General Chuck Yeager zeroed in on when he wrote the tribute to Captain Sullenberger in *Time*. "I don't know Captain 'Sully,'" he said, "and I have only spoken to him briefly, but I am sure that he feels as I do about what he was able to do in a plane: Duty! It was his job."[15]

Duty comes in many forms: emergencies, leadership, giving up your time and freedom to take care of the young or old. For the best public servants—taking care of the greater good is their duty.

In the spring of 2002, Bill Bradley, the former U.S. senator and basketball star, told me, "I want to be a medium." He explained, "I want to be a vehicle for improving the quality of people's lives, whether it's their health, their spiritual well-being, or their economic circumstances. That's where I get the deepest fulfillment—when I'm doing something that actually can improve the quality of life of other human beings." That's Bradley's mission—his reason for being.[16]

Can you imagine if all public officials felt the same duty? How different the world would be.

Mrs. Walton's Litter Patrol

Being dutiful doesn't mean only heroism, leadership, or some kind of selfless mission. Most good, strong individuals lead quiet lives and regularly take on duties, small as well as large.

Mrs. John F. Walton, Jr., whom we first met in chapter 2, was born to privilege, but that didn't keep her from pitching in—literally. More specifically, she picked up other people's litter.

That's right: this esteemed grandmother of sixteen would go to every one of her grandchildren's graduations and very often pick up trash. You know the scene. The ceremony and luncheon are over. People are rushing around saying their good-byes, traffic leaving the parking lot is snarled, and litter is blowing about the campus. Unless she was in conversation, Mrs. Walton could be found bent over, picking up dirty napkins and paper plates. At least one graduation photo album ends with a shot of her smiling wryly as she dropped somebody else's rubbish into a trash bin.

Despite her station, Mrs. Walton was never pretentious or condescending. She never communicated "I'm above this" or "That's not my job." She just pitched in and helped. Even though she once laughingly told a nurse that she'd been "born retired," when she saw a job to be done, she worked.[17]

And it didn't stop there. Event after event, charity after charity, cause after cause, you found her giving. She was a big supporter of the Pittsburgh Symphony while also volunteering at battered women's shelters. If you were at the end of your rope, she was the patient ear on the suicide hotline. This was a woman who felt a duty to give as much as she could.

How You Can Become More Dutiful

If you look around you, if you employ the listening and "absorption" techniques that penetrating realists employ (chapter 8), you'll find an endless array of chores to perform and problems to solve, all of them outside yourself—take your pick. By spending a little time every day focusing your attention on others' needs and figuring out how you can help, you'll find opportunities to effect real change. As with all these traits, it's easiest to start small. Like Mrs. Walton, pick up litter.

Wondering what's in it for you? A lot, including deep psychic connections with others and profound personal fulfillment. You may even get the chance to save someone's life—or 155 lives, as Captain Sullenberger did.

Being dutiful, responsible, and problem focused will inevitably look different to every person. Sometimes it means facing down real enemies, leading despite great uncertainty, or taking big risks—as Andy Grove did in Hungary and then years later when he led Intel. Sometimes it's as tedious as picking up litter. The key is to find ways on a regular basis that you in particular can help. And when you do, you'll find that making the effort is easier. It will be rewarding because by its very nature, helping others gets you outside yourself and in connection with something greater.

Now let's move on to part 4 and the five traits that are your reward for inculcating the first fourteen traits.

Takeaways

The most important ideas to grasp from this chapter are that being dutiful is as gratifying as it is noble and that helping others in small ways, as well as large, is important and puts you on the path to greater service and gratification.

- ✓ Duty is born of a sense of kinship with all humanity.
- ✓ No contribution or bit of honest effort is too small.
- ✓ Duty knows no rank. Think of the Washington, DC, garbage haulers' slogan: "We don't talk trash. We move it!"
- ✓ Help out in areas where you already have desire and skill.
- ✓ Sometimes you have to act more courageous than you feel. But don't fake or oversell your confidence. That can breed doubt.
- ✓ When at risk, think "Keep Calm and Carry On"—from the 1939 poster initially produced by the British Ministry of Information and intended as a "last case scenario" to be used only had the Germans under Hitler succeeded in invading Britain.

Part 4

Earning Your Personal Payoff

Chapter 15

....

Delight in the Day-to-Day

TRAIT: *APPRECIATIVE*

Gratitude is the heart's memory.

—FRENCH PROVERB

THE WALTON FAMILY KNOWS all about the healing and edifying powers of appreciation. It's a trait they've passed down through the generations.

Mrs. John F. Walton, Jr., now deceased, was a superb example of the strongest temperamentally who lived relatively quiet lives. She was born in Pittsburgh, Pennsylvania, in the last year of the nineteenth century and lived well into the twenty-first. She experienced a great deal in her long life, and what she deemed most important were: "love and forgiving those who've wronged you."[1] Hers is a relatively conservative, churchgoing clan, and Mrs. Walton was a devoted Presbyterian. Throughout her life, she took Christian charity to heart and felt a duty to give back—not just money, but time and attention. She was a nurse's aide, an advocate for battered women, and the calm voice of compassion at the end of a crisis hotline.

When she was ninety-nine, I interviewed her on videotape. It was the summer of 1998 and still eight years before she, as the French say, returned to the world of silence.

Mrs. Walton appreciated diversity of thought and faith. She didn't just appreciate others' points of view. She defended them. When I asked her if she believed in God, she replied, "I do. I *really* do. There's something there. We can call it God. Some people call that tree God; others call something else God. And that's our trouble. We get in there and tell the people who believe in the tree that they're all wrong and we're right. And *you can't do that!*"[2]

Mrs. Walton was also appreciative of nature. Indeed, she was in awe of it and relished the simplicity and mystery of all forms of life. For her, even trees could be spiritual beings. "There's life in them," she said to me that day wistfully, "so why not spirit?"[3]

Then she pointed out to the west of her porch on a lake in Canada to a five-foot cedar growing out of a crack in the rocky point that juts out into the dark, fresh water. "You see that little one on the end?" she said with admiration, "it's been there for years. Wouldn't you think it would go down in the winter or when a big storm blows by? But it's there. It's been there for years, just lookin' at us."[4]

That little tree is not the only spirit to weather life's storms. Mrs. Walton's granddaughter and namesake has also been fortified by the mystical and enduring power of wildland. As we saw in chapter 2, the younger Rachel moved to New Mexico, where long walks in the high country helped resuscitate a broken heart.

As a hospice nurse, Rachel sees others' pain and struggle on a daily basis. For most of us, dying is a depressing state of being, a topic that we avoid. For many doctors, nurses, hospital aides, and religious counselors, it's a time of life that offers great psychic rewards, lessons, and gratification. Rachel said, "Seeing others struggle can remind us to be grateful. That's really important. Gratitude is one of the most important qualities because it has to do with the heart. It has to do with being present and not taking the moment for granted. If I put my attention on what I do have, it makes me gratified. And that's good for the world.

"There's always something to be grateful for. Sometimes I think about the fact that I can see. It opens me up. It opens up my vision. I realize all the beauty around me. And when you have that kind of awareness, you start tapping into the heart."[5]

The ability to be still, present, and alert to others, allows you to see all there is to be grateful for. You may be aware of beauty or quiet. You may become aware of pain and confusion. That pain can make you realize your own peace and strength—for which you can and ought to be grateful. Either way, this "tapping into the heart" is another way that exceptional human beings steer and enrich their own lives as well as those of others.

With Rachel's and Poosie Orr's help (chapters 2 and 16), we can understand the real power of appreciation. For instance, Poosie says appreciation is a precursor to love.

And Rachel says appreciation makes her receptive: "When I walk into a patient's room, with their family, I really try to walk in without any assumptions and I let them lead. If you do walk in with assumptions, you miss who that person is and what their needs are. It requires a capacity to be quiet and to listen very carefully . . . I have to not be thinking about other things, not be in a rush, not distracted, not trying to make something happen. As I approach the room, I say to myself, 'Let me hear what needs to be heard, and say what needs to be spoken.'"[6]

Maslow's Take

In *Motivation and Personality*, Maslow notes that "Self-actualizing people have the wonderful capacity to appreciate again and again, freshly and naively, the basic goods of life, with awe, pleasure, wonder, and even ecstasy."[7]

Maslow wasn't treading new terrain here—most books and articles on achieving joy and fulfillment cite the ability to appreciate. The most capable people are grateful too. And while they often have many earthly belongings, they are most gratified by life's regular, simpler blessings, such as good weather, natural surroundings, children, animals, and music.

However, Maslow takes it a large step further by warning that a lack of appreciation for "our blessings is one of the most important nonevil generators of human evil, tragedy, and suffering. What we take for granted we undervalue, and we are therefore too apt to sell a valuable birthright for a mess of pottage."[8] For example, you have no idea where you will be in a year. You may become ill or suffer some financial setback. Someone you love dearly may be gone. Accepting these potential realities can and ought to give you much more appreciation for everything you have right *now*.

One very interesting detail: while Maslow stresses that the strongest among us appreciate the simpler wonders and pleasures of life, he writes that they do not think much of the glitzy, man-made versions. He writes, "No one of them for instance, will get this same sort of reaction from going to a night club or getting a lot of money, or having a good time at a party."[9]

We're all so busy rushing around, trying to compete, earn, and achieve, that we often fail to appreciate the experiences that we all have, especially those that happen with regularity. This is particularly true for those of us lucky enough to be born in free, market-based economies. We have so much to distract us that we rarely take a deep breath and marvel at the life and mystery all around us.

Like Rachel Walton, the hospice nurse, the best human beings are acutely aware of pain and loss, and know that destiny and disease can deal a body blow at any time. This does not make them fearful. It makes them grateful for every day that is healthy and safe. Like animals in the wild, they accept these dangers while being on guard against them. So it makes sublime sense that self-actualizing people appreciate every moment that evil, bad luck, and physical calamity are kept at bay.

How You Can Be More Appreciative

Perhaps most valuable in terms of being more appreciative is simply taking some time each day to be still and setting yourself aside. By this, I mean to be an observer, not an active doer. Best of all is to do this outdoors. There is a lot going on even in a small garden or an apartment balcony. Be a part of it. You may just experience wind and sound. But if you suspend all your earthly, manufactured concerns, what Joseph Campbell calls "creative incubation" will take place.[10]

Understanding others' faiths can deepen yours and give you more perspective on your own beliefs. The best-selling author and psychiatrist M. Scott Peck believed that the psychologically healthy are usually more advanced spiritually because not only are they tolerant of other faiths, but they are also open to the mysteries and even the miracles of faith. This is startling because these are fact-based decision makers. They usually do not put much value in blind adherence to ritual and rule. But because they also understand how little humankind actually knows about physics, other dimensions, energy, and the universe, they are open to the possibilities of much, *much* more going on.

This kinship with all humankind also makes the good among the great curious and appreciative of others' ways. Because they're experiential (chapter 7), they often enter the temples and delve into others' belief systems and rituals. Not only will appreciating the unknown help you see the forest and not just the trees, it will also help you recognize that some forests are enchanted.

As we learned in chapter 9, the good among the great are drawn to, not repelled by, the mysterious. The best people are very often comfortable with and even excited by adventure, what's yet to be discovered, and possibility.

Exceptional individuals also appreciate the mere idea of spirit, whether within themselves, within others, or in the ether. They have a tacit understanding that whatever animates our bodies may be on a never-ending journey of discovery, including the development of our own spirits. And one person who can help us explore that mystery is the late Reverend R. Maurice Boyd.

The Reverend Maurice Boyd on Discerning and Appreciating What Is Truly Valuable

The Reverend R. Maurice Boyd was born in Northern Ireland. A fervent Protestant, he moved to Canada and in London, Ontario, he attracted one of the largest congregations in the country. Soon he was recruited to New York City to head Fifth Avenue Presbyterian Church, one of America's preeminent Presbyterian congregations. After three years, he left to found the City Church, where he had time and freedom to develop powerful sermons drawn from poetry, literature, and philosophy as well as scripture.

One of Boyd's most enduring sermon themes was a passionate plea that all of us wake up to the precious time that is our lives. "The terrible thing is that people realize too late that many of the things they're going after don't keep their promises. For me, a perfect definition of hell is to have everything you've ever wanted . . . and still not be satisfied, to know that you've missed something."[11]

In Boyd's faith and analysis, human beings can't help but feel the separation from and anticipation of something much bigger. "I think the whole pilgrimage is a kind of journey between lost content and heart's desire. We're moving all the time from one kind of longing to looking for another kind of satisfaction."[12]

Echoing Dr. Andrew Weil (chapter 1), Boyd went on, "I'm not a temporal being moving toward the eternal; I am an eternal being moving for a little while in the temporal. That's the truth about me. That's the truth about all people. If you don't see that, then you miss the deepest thing about you."[13]

Fully Appreciating Your Senses

For Poosie Orr, the best place to appreciate glimpses of eternity is on the wonderful Canadian lake to which I've referred in Ontario, Canada. This is a large body of fresh water, filled with fish and loon, and dotted with rocky, pine-covered islands. While it freezes every winter, the water is warm every summer. Poosie's place has been in her late husband's family for six generations. "Canada is beautiful," Poosie said. "It has a quietness that is so welcome these days." Not only is Poosie an expert practitioner of lifelong love, she's also a master of appreciating the smaller, priceless things in life. To do so, she feels the need to "get alone and away from all the clattering and claptrap . . . When you go down to your dock at night and the boats aren't out, you look at the stars and it's so peaceful. That's a *gift*. It's a gift to have a place like that, instead of a wild weekend. When you look around this house you can tell: it's where we came together. We all share this incredible space we've inherited. It's part of our roots."[14]

On this part of the lake, there are almost no commercial places to go at night, and most people still don't have televisions or even radios. So families play games, read, build things, and catch up on sleep. "We all know that there are no places to go," Poosie said. "And who *wants* to go out at night? So we sit by the fire and read. That's a giant, giant gift."[15]

For Poosie, even the shared sounds are something to be grateful for. "Lots of us had tapes made of Canada sounds: the screen door closing, the boat starting up, the loons. Even the plumbing noises! And don't forget the pine forest smells. It's not just the sights and it's not just the quiet. It gets you in all the senses . . . And then family! We're so lucky we have so many generations of friends. The generational connections are unbelievable. That's so important because there's this background going way back of people loving exactly the same thing."[16]

I asked Poosie how she could continue to have such a fresh appreciation for something that she had experienced over and over again. "Because it still goes on," she replied, without missing a beat. "It's a continuation. I'll tell you a story . . . we used to always go camping at night out at a small, pristine, neighboring lake. One year, when the kids were very little, they made a line of little fairy houses out of moss and acorns, out by the cabin there. I remember going back the next year and looking to see, and sure enough—the same little village with the little acorns and the little trees was right where they'd left it. It was still there. *You can't beat that!*"[17]

Appreciation takes presence, and presence takes slowing down. If you're a busy high achiever, give yourself a break from the world of humans, take a deep breath, and open yourself to what you can sense, what you do not know, and what could be. You'll begin to notice so many precious gifts that don't demand your attention. By keeping your attention focused outward, you can gently remind yourself how lucky you are and how little you know and how much more there is to explore. That can open you up so that more can come in. Just what might come in, coming up!

Takeaways

Being appreciative or grateful for what you have and the simpler, natural elements of life will not only make you happier but also provide a gateway to more love, adventure, and spiritual exploration.

✓ Embrace that much is unknown—notably your future. Be drawn into life's mysteries and you will be not only more aware, but also wise and appreciative.

✓ Be grateful that while much of life is not in your control, much is.

✓ Appreciate what you don't know, how much you can learn, and how much remains a mystery—and in that lies great possibility, hope, and risk.

✓ Regularly take ten minutes to be outside. While you're out, fully engage each and every one of your senses and appreciate those natural things that delight you.

✓ Prayer starts with appreciation. A simple thank-you works wonders.

✓ Do not put much value in blind adherence to religious ritual and rule.

✓ Understand how little humankind actually knows about physics, other dimensions, energy, and the universe, so that you are open to the possibilities of much, *much* more going on.

Chapter 16

··

Go Out and Play

TRAIT: *CREATIVE*

*The creation of something new is not
accomplished by the intellect but by the play
instinct acting from inner necessity. The creative
mind plays with the objects it loves.*

—C. G. JUNG

JULIA CAMERON IS NO stranger to the public eye.
She caused a sensation twenty years ago when she wrote *The Artist's Way*. Today, the book has sold more than two million copies worldwide, solidifying Cameron's position as the authority on
"creative unblocking." But what most people don't know about
Cameron is the darker side of her past—the part that came before
the book.

As a student at Georgetown University, Cameron's nightly
routine included writing at bars, drinking doubles, and experi-

encing serious memory blackouts. Even as a high school senior, she was, in her own words, "a bad girl waiting to happen."[1] After graduating, she became a hard-drinking journalist at the *Washington Post*, followed by a stint at *Rolling Stone*. It was the latter appointment that led her to interview filmmaker Martin Scorsese. It must have been a stimulating interchange. They married in 1975.

In Los Angeles, Cameron added cocaine to the cocktail of drugs and alcohol that kept her going. With the success of *Taxi Driver*, Scorsese was suddenly the new celebrity in town, and they were both swept up in a frenetic, privacy-robbing tide of fame. Their marriage was turbulent and lonely. In her memoir *Floor Sample*, Cameron confessed, "Without my writing to anchor me, I was fragile and storm-tossed. In a town that names credits before the arrest, my sole credit was being Martin's wife. I spiraled further and further into alcoholism and drug addiction, alone in the house on the hill."[2]

Two years later, in the wake of Cameron's continued descent into alcoholism and Scorsese's well-publicized affair with Liza Minelli, the marriage was over. Cameron and Scorsese had collaborated on three films and one beloved, extracurricular project: their daughter, Domenica.

The early years were hard. Cameron wound up in New York on assignment, somehow managing to write between blackouts, paranoia, and cocaine-induced highs. She had brief bouts of sobriety, but celebrity parties still held their glamorous allure. Existing without them—and without Scorsese—didn't seem like enough. In the meantime, Cameron was trying to juggle single parenthood between New York, Los Angeles, and Taos, New Mexico, rushing from one place to the next at breakneck speed.

And "breakneck" was right. Around this time, Cameron's Alcohoholics Anonymous sponsor gave her a chart of forty-three alcoholic symptoms. She had experienced forty-one. Finally, Cameron could no longer sustain her internal tug of war. Between writing and drinking, one had to go. So she foreswore drugs and alcohol and began going on daily walks in the Hollywood Hills. "Walking, I discovered, was good for me as a writer. A footfall at a time, I came to clarity about plot and character. Sometimes I would rush home, eager to get to the page."[3]

Her sober mentors told her, "You're a writer and writers write, and it is the writing that makes you a writer."[4]

Cameron tried out this theory, first on a small scale. She set a quota for herself: three pages a day. It was not only recovery from alcoholism but also to creativity. Later, this idea of daily writing quotas would make her famous. And in her personal life, it worked wonders. Over a decade passed before Cameron published *The Artist's Way*, but once she began teaching creative unblocking, her destiny was found. The book was an international success, inspiring people all over the globe to recover their artistic impulses. "My books are not creative theory," she explained. "They spring straight out of my own creative practice. In a sense, I am the floor sample of my own tool kit. When we are unblocked we can have remarkable and diverse adventures."[5]

For Cameron, those adventures have taken her in many different directions—all far from the world of addiction. Today she is not only a prominent author but a teacher, artist, poet, playwright, novelist, filmmaker, composer, and journalist.

Cameron's road to recovered creativity has led to professional pursuits. For most of us, recovered creativity simply leads to joyous personal pursuits.

All we have to do is learn how to play again—how to relax; quiet the nagging, demanding, judging voice in our minds; unblock our spirits; and work more from sensation, feelings, and maybe something external. As Cameron put it, "I wasn't so much writing as I was eavesdropping. I wasn't so much thinking something up as taking something down."[6]

Getting something "down" is fundamental to becoming a happier, healthier, more productive human being. In this chapter, we'll see why and learn how.

Maslow's Take

According to Abraham Maslow, a "universal characteristic" of what he called "self-actualizing" or very healthy individuals psychologically is that they are more creative than most people. More specifically, they have "recovered" an unspoiled child's creativity.[7]

Maslow believed that we are all born creative people, that creativity is second nature to us. This creativity manifests itself in obvious ways during our childhoods—we invent games, talk to imaginary friends, and give personalities to trees and animals. We build entire neighborhoods with building blocks and if allowed, draw on everything. Then, somewhere along the way, we're hemmed in, routinized, restricted. We're judged, often harshly, and we learn to disrespect and even mistrust our native impulses, pushing them to the side to make way for the pressures and demands of our analytical, left-brain world.

In keeping with Cameron's theme of recovery, Maslow believed that exceptional adults *recover* their natural creativity by unleashing the unadulterated person within. They are "less inhibited, less constricted, less bound, in a word, less enculturated."[8]

These individuals aren't necessarily world-class violinists or sculptors. Their output doesn't have to be grandiose. Maslow notes that their creative efforts are often of a humble nature. They find expression for their creativity in simple pursuits, such as cooking, gardening, dancing, singing, and photography. Whether playing a musical instrument, setting a table, or just writing a letter, they do it with ability and originality.

An abundance of creative energy is characteristic of psychological health. We've seen the evidence throughout history. Winston Churchill painted. Abraham Lincoln was a great story- and joke-teller. Thomas Jefferson designed buildings and furniture. So many entrepreneurs I've interviewed cook and garden in truly inventive ways. And their homes are always of singular design.

Although few in number, some organizations are designed for and devoted to taking high achievers into the creative realm. For example, the Bohemian Grove has a 2,700-acre campground that belongs to a private, somewhat secretive San Francisco–based men's club. Each summer, the Grove hosts a three-week extravaganza on its grounds for business leaders, media executives, and even government officials—some of the most powerful men in the world. Reportedly, the events feature a wide spectrum of performances, everything from environmental talks to drag shows and stage antics from people like former secretary of state George Shultz and former president George H. W. Bush.

Participation in the creative process is highly encouraged, if not mandatory at the Grove. The specific goal is to suspend the analytical mind-set and evolve through performance. If you can't sing, dance, or act, then grab a hammer: you're going to help build a set. I think organizations like the Grove are desperately needed in every capital in the world. Creative play would make for more creative leadership.

Michael Giacchino's Creative Plea to Children

At the 2010 Academy Awards, one acceptance speech stood out from the rest. It wasn't given by an A-list celebrity. In fact, it came from a man most of us had never heard of, from a guy who, like Maslow, feels that kids are creative and they just need some encouragement to stay that way. That man was Michael

Giacchino, the composer who penned the musical score for the Disney film *Up*.

Giacchino's speech was simple but powerful. "Thank you, guys," he began.

> When I was nine, I asked my dad, "Can I have your movie camera? That old, wind-up 8-millimeter camera that's in your drawer?"
>
> And he goes, "Sure, take it."
>
> And I took it, and I started making movies with it, and I started being as creative as I could. And not once in my life did my parents ever say, "What you're doing is a waste of time." Never. And I grew up, and I had teachers, I had colleagues—I had people that I worked with all through my life who always told me, "What you're doing is not a waste of time." So it was normal to me that it was okay to do that.
>
> I know there are kids out there that don't have that support system, so if you're out there and you're listening, listen to me: If you want to be creative, get out there and do it. It's not a waste of time. Do it. Okay? Thank you. Thank you.[9]

That creative urge is exactly what Maslow is talking about—and what's more, this man actually went on to make a profession out of it. Giacchino didn't recover his creativity because he never lost it in the first place. He held on to his love for film and music throughout his childhood and passionately pursued it as he got older. One Emmy, three Grammys, one Golden Globe, and an Academy Award later, he's the epitome of success.

How You Can Recover Some Creativity—Be Hands On

In the Orr household, which also had plenty of books and games, were boxes and bags filled with materials to build and paint things. And the family members all painted as well as constructed models and mobiles. Their wonderful old lake cottage today has homemade toys and contraptions scattered on shelves and hanging from ceilings. For Poosie, the Orr family matriarch, an emphasis on creativity is fundamental.

"In my book," she said, "it's *very* important that people use their hands somehow. I think we're meant to. Whether we're painting or cooking or sewing or digging, I just think there's something very vital about using your hands."[10]

For Poosie, one of the most wonderful facets of the creative process is just that: the process. "I feel very sorry for some people—and I've known a few—who appreciate the finished, perfected thing. Those people often buy the things they like: the sleek, finished product. And they're very pleased they could buy it. But boy, that doesn't beat *making* it."[11]

Like Michael Giacchino, Poosie Orr was fortunate enough to grow up in a household that encouraged and nurtured her creative instincts. She remembers making all kinds of items as a child—paper dolls, kites, a slingshot. And it didn't stop in childhood; Poosie thinks it's even *more* important to exercise our creative impulse as adults. Why?

"Because it keeps you going and you have *fun*. I just got a quote from a friend the other day: 'If you have a talent, use it. Because the forest won't grow if only the best birds sing.' So, use it! Because it's a God-given thing. Everybody's basically creative."[12]

According to Poosie, people who think they don't have a creative bone in their bodies just weren't given the right encouragement or opportunities. Maybe they were stifled by parents who said, "Oh, don't let her paint—she'll mess up the room." Poosie, on the other hand, always encouraged her children to use their creativity to the utmost. Today, her four grown kids as well as their spouses and children still give each other a handmade present every Christmas.

Then there's Andrew Ferguson, the former Teach for America teacher and current law student we met in chapter 11. Ferguson's mother encouraged his creativity when he was growing up. Because he and his brother chose to bunk in one room, their mom set aside an extra bedroom for building blocks—hundreds, maybe thousands, of them. Every day, Ferguson would come home from school and build with his brother.

Twenty years later, he launched a similar experiment in the trailer at L. W. Beecher Elementary School. To teach his students geometry, he divided the boys into groups of four, and purchased each group over thirty feet of wood from Home Depot. Then he put all the lumber in the middle of the room.

The class was on "3-D shapes, angles, measurements, and all that good stuff," said Ferguson. "So rather than using textbooks, we spent two weeks where I had this huge pile of wood, hammers, saws, nails—you name it. I explained that I wanted a building four feet tall that could stand without falling over. 'Beyond that,' I said, 'it's up to you!'"[13]

Ferguson strung up caution tape to create a work zone atmosphere, and then he stepped back as the boys got to work. He admitted to being a little hesitant at first, seeing as how most of his inner-city students had never picked up a hammer or a saw. A lot of them smacked their thumbs on their very first try. But the end result was worth the sore thumbs.

"It was fantastic," Ferguson declared, "how they all worked well on a team—sawing things, holding things for each other. They didn't have workbenches, so it was difficult. But it was a fantastic teamwork experience. At the end, all but one of the sixteen teams had a building over four feet tall, most of which were five to five and a half feet tall: strong buildings that they spray-painted. It was a terrific experience."[14]

From building blocks to building buildings, Andrew has found innovative ways to bring out the creative impulse that lurks within us all.

Practice Spiritual Creativity

How are or were you creative? How can you channel your innate creativity in ways that enhance your day-to-day existence?

We may be tempted to focus on the *product* of our creative endeavors rather than the *process*. But as Muriel Maffre and Poosie Orr attest, the two aren't mutually exclusive. In fact, sometimes you can derive the greater pleasure from the creative process itself.

Take Rachel Walton, the nurse whom we've already met. For Rachel, creativity is about focusing and taking a break from oneself—and it's a source of delight.

"I am constantly finding ways to be creative," she said. "I play with water colors, I bead, knit, put flowers on the table, and write letters to people. These are very important for me. They are another function of the heart—an activity where I need to slow down and allow it to happen."[15]

Rachel's forays into the artistic realm are not about thinking or the end result. "I don't need to make something . . . to have a product. It's the process that is helpful. When I sit down with my pastels and take an hour or two to do it, it's very quieting. It's very focused too. It's almost like what meditation practice would give to somebody. I'm connecting to that and appreciating it."[16]

If creativity is something we're all born with—a great, shared part of being human—and the quality of what we do create is somehow out of our hands, something to which we connect, then we have to acknowledge that some element of it is beyond us. It's not so much about what we do or make; it may be more about what we allow to happen or whom we invite in. Many artists agree with the notion that a great creative work is not generated by the individual artist. That something else comes into play, or rather works through the individual—call it the wind, a muse, the gods, or what you will.

In his weekly sermons at the City Church of New York, the Reverend R. Maurice Boyd would often quote some writer who said, "I want to be a house that is haunted."[17] Our job is to humble ourselves, do the work, and allow space for that haunting, whatever or whoever may haunt us.

Happy, healthy human beings know how to invite, tap, or release that energy. Doing so makes them exuberant, joyous, and open to more transcendent or peak experiences—which happen to be the final, three thrilling traits that we explore in this book.

Takeaways

You can and ought to recover the boundless creative energy that you had as a child. Doing so not only quiets our overused analytical minds, it's fun and allows you to rediscover the joys of process—the delight in doing.

✓ Find quiet time alone regularly, daily if this is new to you. As Joseph Campbell said in the PBS series *The Power of Myth*, "You must have a room, or a certain hour or so a day, where you don't know what was in the newspapers that morning, you don't know who your friends are, you don't know what you owe anybody, you don't know what anybody owes to you. This is a place where you can simply experience and bring forth what you are and what you might be. This is the place of creative incubation. At first you may find that nothing happens there. But if you have a sacred place and use it, something eventually will happen."[18]

✓ Encourage and participate in artistic endeavors, no matter how simple.

✓ Keep a notepad or recorder in the car. Ideas often come when you're driving.

✓ Sensory experience suspends analytical thinking and spurs creativity. Take a hot shower, go outdoors, take a long walk, swim, or immerse yourself in nature.

✓ Schedule time for daydreaming and time with no purpose.

✓ If you have children, grandchildren, or pets—let them choose the game or activity and encourage them to create games of their own making.

✓ Change your routine routinely.

✓ Use your hands.

✓ Think of the creative process as one of allowing rather than doing.

Chapter 17

Shout Out Loud!

TRAIT: *EXUBERANT*

Exuberance is beauty.

—WILLIAM BLAKE

DOES YOUR BOSS INSIST that you party? Jack Welch does.

As the former chairman and CEO of GE, Welch was my boss when I worked at CNBC. In 2001, after I'd left the business channel, I had the chance to interview him for the third time, and that dialogue remains one of my all-time favorites to this day.

"I think business is a lot about spirit," Welch declared. "When I think of spirit I think of energy, of excitement. I think of exciting others. What's worse than a manager who sits around and *manages* people? This is all about exciting people and making it more fun!"[1]

Welch gets indignant at the idea that formality is part of big business "Formality is the killer of business! *Informality* is what makes a company work—when the quality of an idea is not measured by the level in the organizational box, but only by the quality of the idea. This isn't just about first-name stuff. This is about being able to try things, wing things. This is about being able to celebrate."[2]

"Companies have a tough time celebrating," Welch went on, really gathering steam. "I mean, every little victory—a ratings win at CNBC—get a keg, throw a party. *Do something!* This is where you spend your *life*! Have a ball at it. Why would you want to come to a place as a stuffed shirt and hang around a corporation? It's dumb—unless you had a ball!"[3]

Welch isn't just pushing keg parties. He's pushing something far more vital and fantastic: *spontaneous exuberance.*

These days, we're so overscheduled that often we can't find time to be spontaneous. Victory drinks? Not tonight, we won't find a sitter at this hour. Congratulatory gala? Sure—do you have a free Thursday evening after Memorial Day? It's hard to be exuberant on a schedule. Scheduling a celebration in the future for a piece of great news today defeats the point. Good fortune requires recognition at the moment of awareness.

This is where children are superior to adults. Kids have no qualms about immediately expressing their glee—shouting, giggling, and dancing without a second thought. This is where young athletes with their leaping, hooting, and chest bumping know the score. This is where Meryl Streep's portrayal of Julia Child in *Julie and Julia* with her loud "oooohs" and delighted squeals, got it right. Spontaneity is a key ingredient of joy, and it's an outgrowth of an integrated, unguarded, joyous personality.

Maslow's Take

In *Motivation and Personality*, Maslow notes that creative self-actualizing people tend to see the world with clear, "innocent" eyes, with an "uninhibited spontaneity and expressiveness."[4]

Enter Jack Welch.

"When I talk to these managers three levels down," Welch nearly threatened, "I say 'Your job as a leader is to go around and pump self-confidence into people so they feel six feet tall with hair!'"[5]

Welch, of course, is about five-foot-six and bald, but no one can argue that he stands as a giant among business leaders. And he tops just about everybody when it comes to expressing himself and having a lot of fun while making a lot of money—for himself and others.

The success story of John Francis Welch, Jr., is the stuff of American dreams and has a lot to do with Welch's personality and specifically his expressive, infectious passion. His parents were middle-class folk from Worcester, Massachusetts—his father was a train conductor and his mom, a housewife. Welch points to his mother's parenting style as one of the formative factors in his success. She endlessly encouraged and simultaneously demanded more from him, telling him that his talents were large and his faults were really strengths in disguise. For instance, she convinced him that he stuttered because his mouth couldn't keep up with his brain.

We now know that this wasn't just a mother's pride talking. Welch's talents *were* large—large enough to see him become GE's youngest chairman and CEO at the age of forty-six. Over the next twenty years, GE's market value spiked from $14 billion to more than $410 billion, making it one of the most valuable and largest companies in the world.[6]

GE's growth defied all predictions. One key reason was its finance unit, which powered profit growth. But that single division can't explain GE's stunning twenty-year record under Welch. By the 1980s, conglomerates like GE were supposed to sag under their own complexity. But Welch understood a simple truth about business and human nature—that he could make a huge, far-flung collection of businesses work if he focused on the one common denominator in all GE's various pursuits: people. Not many know that Welch spent over half his time on human resources issues. Understand that for most CEOs, HR is a bit of a backwater. Yet Welch spent the majority of his time huddled with his HR team, hiring, coaching, testing, grading, incentivizing, disciplining, firing, and—you guessed it— *celebrating* his workers. I've never seen a boss more adept at rewarding and cheering on the people who work for him.

Welch did it on a large-scale, systemic basis—gathering managers from disparate GE divisions to analyze and challenge each other on their strategies. At the GE education facility in Crotonville, New York, he would also have lower-level executives critique their bosses. Instinctively, he demonstrated a healthy person's trait of exuberant expressiveness on a corporate-wide basis. But Welch also did it on a personal basis. One of the world's busiest humans, he (as President George H. W. Bush did) still took the time nearly every evening to pen short notes of encouragement to the people who worked for him.

Be More Childlike

I interviewed several of Jack Welch's childhood buddies, and they all describe vividly his leadership style as a boy in "the Pit," an old gravel pit in which they played sports. He was a fierce competitor and fearless in his defense of fair play—even when competing with older boys. His leadership style at GE was the same. The boyish exuberance lived on in the man. This is not unusual among the best people I've encountered.

If this kind of spirit seems too hard to unleash, remember that we all started out with that kind of genuine, spontaneous exuberance. But then, somewhere along the way, it gets reeled back in and bottled up. Most of us lose this wonderful ability to show ourselves emotionally and sincerely. As adults, we slip into routines that no longer excite us. (See chapter 1 for guidance on how the good among the great continually chart their own paths to higher and more relevant purpose.) Doing so makes their lives exciting. We also compartmentalize our lives to such a degree that we often have to remind ourselves how to let go.

How You Can Be More Exuberant

Do you have a hard time having fun, letting go at a party? A lot of hard-core, ambitious executives do. I submit that at work and in particular on social and family occasions, you ought to consider it part of your job to have fun.

Reward yourself and those around you for good work. Jack Welch did and he insisted that you do it immediately.

If you enjoy singing and dancing or telling jokes, then do so more often. Even the worst dancers are often admired if they do so with abandon!

If you're unconvinced that it's important to really relax and play as an adult, then let me give you a great reason why it is important—being genuine, expressive, and spontaneous is very appealing to others. Therefore it's an important quality that will attract followers to your cause. Another reason is that it's reassuring to others when you let down your guard. And it's particularly refreshing in a world populated with fakes, climbers, and salespeople. Being exuberant is the outward display of someone who's not only passionate but comfortable enough in his or her own skin to show it.

Those who live authentic, expressive lives are magnetic, powerful, and infectious personalities. If you can't have fun then others will wonder how whole you are, even how true you are, and they're less apt to be attracted to you or your ideas.

Become more charismatic by being more exuberant.

Takeaways

The principal lesson here is that while the good among the great can come across as cool or aloof when you first meet them, they are very often enthusiastic, even childlike in their expressive spontaneity. This personality trait can be indicative of many characteristics, including an integrated, whole person who is unguarded when around those he or she trusts and who is also very likely joyous.

- ✓ Celebrate surprises and successes immediately!
- ✓ Don't restrain your children when their rambunctiousness is harmless. Indeed, find a time and place every day to let them be loud, boisterous, and free to express themselves.
- ✓ Observe and participate in games and creative and physical pursuits.
- ✓ If the mood strikes, party. If it doesn't, don't.
- ✓ Dance, and do so with abandon.
- ✓ Learn to edit your thinking and talking less. It may shake up your relationships. But maybe they need shaking up.

....

Chapter 18

Dive into What You Love

TRAIT: *JOYOUS*

I always tell my students, go where your body and soul want to go. When you have the feeling, then stay with it, and don't let anyone throw you off.

—JOSEPH CAMPBELL

"I HAVE PASSION," SHELLY Lazarus said. "I love what I do and don't undersell that *ever* as a quality. People respond to passionate people."[1] In an industry that is full of drama queens and one-shot wonders, people have gravitated to Shelly Lazarus. She's got the accolades and longevity to prove it. Now the chairman of Ogilvy & Mather Worldwide, she has been a leader at the storied agency for decades. She started as an account executive when most women were still relegated to the secretarial pool, and she advanced through the ranks in a series of promotions that landed her the top spot: chief executive officer.

Like many good people who ascend to powerful positions, Lazarus still doesn't quite believe that she deserves it. "I had no ambitions when I started out. I mean my whole life was sort of an accident. I fell into marketing, I fell into advertising, I fell into Ogilvy. I never intended to stay more than two years. I just thought it would be a good idea to spend two years at an ad agency.

"I stumbled my way to the top. It's absolutely true. I just sort of found something I loved to do and I just kept doing it. And every once in a while someone would come along and put a new title on my head. Either I lack self-confidence or I have humility but every time it was always a *surprise* to me and I always felt I wasn't ready. It was 'No! *I* can't do that job.'"[2]

Yes! She certainly could and did. As chairman and CEO, Lazarus spearheaded a series of campaigns that catapulted the game of brand building to a new level. Dove, IBM, Johnson & Johnson, American Express, Kraft, Kodak—a wide variety of companies owe at least part of their reputations and sales to the acumen of Shelly Lazarus and her team at Ogilvy. She has been named Advertising Woman of the Year, received a Distinguished Leadership Award from Columbia Business School, and was ranked in *Fortune*'s "50 Most Powerful Women in Business" for ten years running. Though Lazarus stepped down from her position as CEO in 2008, she is still the chairman and an active member of Ogilvy & Mather Worldwide—not to mention the face people attach to the company name.

Now in her early sixties, Lazarus seems as dynamic as ever. I interviewed her in late February 2010 at Ogilvy headquarters in New York, and the experience was like reminiscing with your favorite teacher—the one who inspired you and convinced you that you could achieve anything. At the end of the interview, the cameramen, the producers—everybody in the room—were beaming. Lazarus is so genuine and down to earth that you don't feel as if you're being sold anything. The irony, of course, is that she's a master salesperson.

"You have to keep life in perspective," she said with a grin. "I mean advertising is advertising."[3]

Lazarus's humility as well as her exuberance are no doubt key reasons for her success as a wife, a mother, and a leader in an industry where not only do clients have to trust you, they have to *like* you. As a CEO, Lazarus had to be a shrewd judge of character, a master at organizational politics, and a tough boss when she needed to be, and yet virtually everyone who's ever crossed her path speaks to her charisma, warmth, and enthusiasm. She is, simply put, a joyous human being and, for the most part, always has been.

Indeed, pursuing happiness has played a vital part in virtually all Shelly Lazarus's life choices. In Joanne Gordon's book *Be Happy at Work: 100 Women Who Love Their Jobs, and Why*, Lazarus shares how she chose a college in the 1960s. "Women couldn't get into Yale and Harvard at the time, so if you were smart and capable and academically strong, you attended an all-women's college like Smith, which I did. I picked Smith because it was the happiest campus I visited. There was so much energy. The women were warm and caring and fun and capable."[4]

And pursuing happiness is not just for Lazarus herself. She believed and still believes it ought to be a driving principle for everyone. Thirty-seven years later, Shelly Lazarus returned to Smith College to deliver the commencement address to the class of 2005.

The question for you is not, "Can you have it all?" The question for you is, "What do you really want? How can you have a life where you enjoy everything in it?"

Can you have a life where you enjoy almost everything in it? *Absolutely!* I know so. But first, you must jettison the things that just don't matter, the things that don't engage you, the things that don't have meaning to you. And then take every ounce of energy you have and dive into what you love.

There is a great truth that I have learned on my journey: you will always be able to fit into your life all the things you love. It's the tedious and the frustrating that are hard to fit in. And you shouldn't even try.[5]

Do you hear echoes of Andrew Ferguson when he said that he "thoroughly enjoyed" teaching disadvantaged children and Warren Buffett when he described how he "tap dances" to work? Are you reminded of Poosie Orr's philosophy of parenting, "You want [your children] to have fun!" or Jack Welch's directive to "have a ball!" Extending this approach to life and work is American at its core. But I also think it's profoundly healthy and energizing. I also expect that it will spread globally and will become very much part of the future in many countries as they raise their living standards. Not only are all kinds of places unleashing their citizens to make money in newly reformed market economies, they are also building societies that are stable and bountiful enough for individuals, particularly young people, to elevate their sights beyond subsistence—where they can do what they really want and love to do.

Doing what they love will make people more joyous, and it could spur a global acceleration in productivity, since those who are joyously engaged on a daily basis produce more and better work.

Maslow's Take

In his book *Toward a Psychology of Being*, Abraham Maslow says that "there are subjective confirmations or reinforcements of self-actualization or of good growth toward it. These are the feelings of zest in living, of happiness or euphoria, of serenity, of joy."[6] In other words, self-actualizing people are well aware that they're on the right track because not only are they succeeding, they're happy.

There's a reason people like Shelly Lazarus feel the zest in living that they do. Like the army's advertising slogan, one critical element to joy is to "be all you can be." Every person's job in life is to be oneself well. Not that everyone's purpose is to "excel" or "be kind" or "think globally and act locally" or any other bit of bumper sticker wisdom. It's simply to be all *you* can be. It's very close to Joseph Campbell's advice to all his college students, "Follow your bliss." Doing so will, in all likelihood, make you joyful.

In other words, clearly know your goals but also focus on the "doing," not just the goal. This is one of the most important and wonderful messages of this book—happiness *ought* to be pursued!

However, it's both easier and tougher than you might think. Being joyous and enthusiastic every day means you have to be *doing* what you truly want to do and *being* who you are truly meant to be. Setting yourself up in a life that suits you requires the reflection and wisdom to know and accept yourself first and then the courage to pursue your own path. That's the true definition of wisdom—not just knowing the right choice but acting on it. That takes autonomy and preparation and courage.

"It's the Key to Success on Every Level"

In 2009, Lazarus gave the commencement speech at Smeal College of Business at the Pennsylvania State University. Though world events necessitated that she address the business implications of the economic crisis, the positive core of her message hadn't changed from her address four years earlier.

I want to add just one piece of personal advice before I end. It is the single most important lesson I have learned in my career. And it is simply: Please, please do something you love.

Life is short. Go find the things that you find exciting, important, intellectually stimulating.

I think finding real fulfillment and joy . . . is the ultimate challenge you face because it's the key to success on every level. People who succeed tend to love what they do. People who succeed in finding balance in their lives always love what they do.[7]

Joyous Ice Cream Makers: Ben and Jerry

Ben Cohen and Jerry Greenfield of Ben & Jerry's Homemade Ice Cream are two good-humored, aging hippies who violated every rule of business and still became ice cream kings. Like Shelly Lazarus, they joyously admit that they stumbled their way to the top.

I profiled these unlikely food moguls back in 2001 for an episode of a television series titled *Great Leaders*. Neither had a detailed career plan except to never be business leaders. Their wacky, happy partnership actually began in the seventh grade, when they bonded as the slowest kids in gym class. When they grew up, Ben first wanted to be a potter, but no one would buy his pots. And Jerry wanted to be a doctor, but he couldn't get into medical school. Together, they fell back on food because they both loved to eat, and they ended up opening an ice cream parlor in an abandoned gas station simply because they didn't have enough money for a bagel shop.

Ben became the master taster because he has no sense of smell. Since a person's sense of taste is partly reliant on his or her sense of smell Ben and Jerry felt that if they could concoct an ice cream that could impress Ben's compromised sense of taste, they would be on to something. This forced Jerry to make the richest and chunkiest ice cream so that Ben could identify the flavors with his eyes closed. This wacky approach to product development worked, and within a few years they were selling $3 million worth of ice cream annually. The future looked bright, but both Ben and Jerry hated their jobs. "We're '60s kids!" Jerry declared. "For us, business had a lot of negative connotations."[8]

Ben and Jerry made plans to sell their promising startup until a sage old friend told them that if they didn't like the way business was done, they could pioneer a new way of doing business. So, Ben and Jerry decided to do what would make them happy, and they embraced several corporate missions, including purity standards, worker protections, contributions to local charities, and even restriction of the sale of their stock to Vermont residents.

Just like Shelly Lazarus, they crafted daily routines where they got to do only what they wanted to do: Ben worked on sales and marketing. Jerry handled production. And they laugh, "No one handled the books! We weren't good bosses."[9]

Somehow, they muddled along until 2000, when they sold their groundbreaking business to Dutch giant Unilever for $326 million.

All their success and pioneering business practices flow from a single choice they made very early on—to do what they love and to love what they do. And it's still a surprise even for them, said Jerry, "We're pretty shocked at what the company has accomplished, and as I've said many times, the people who know us are even more shocked!"[10]

Takeaways

Joy comes from following your heart. It's also a natural outgrowth of success in life, which is aided by adopting the other eighteen personality traits in this book. And being deeply joyous feeds back into the other traits—reinforcing them in a virtuous circle.

- ✓ Believe the Declaration of Independence. "The pursuit of happiness" is a great and good goal itself.

- ✓ Abandon the precept that success requires continuous, great sacrifice. The healthiest among us, wrote Maslow, have a "healthy selfishness, a great self-respect, a disinclination to make sacrifices without good reason."[11]

- ✓ Resist detailed career planning. Allow yourself to stumble to the top by doing what you want to do—the way Shelly Lazarus as well as Ben Cohen and Jerry Greenfield did.

- ✓ The question is not, "Can you have it all?" The question is, "What do you really want, and what really makes you happy?"

- ✓ Life is short. Don't waste a breath on things or people that are tedious and irritating.

Chapter 19

Take a Peak

TRAIT: *TRANSCENDENT*

The sense of self dissolves into an awareness of a greater unity.

—ABRAHAM MASLOW

IN NOVEMBER 2000, TWO women set out to make history. Ann Bancroft, formerly a Minnesota schoolteacher, was joined by Norwegian explorer Liv Arnesen on the coldest, driest, windiest terrain on earth. Together, the women attempted to snow sail and cross-country ski across Antarctica, its landmass and surrounding ice pack, during the Antarctic summer—some seventeen hundred miles. They were not just the first women to attempt this; they were the first humans.

The journey wasn't without its perils. A few years earlier when Arnesen trekked solo much of the same route to the South Pole, she crashed through thin ice onto a ledge just above a deep crevasse. She barely caught herself on the ledge and avoided near-certain death. On this trip, Arnesen fell again into a crevasse, this time one so deep the bottom disappeared into the dark distance. Bancroft tore her right shoulder muscle, making each mile a painful test of endurance. In Antarctica, even the smallest mistake—like accidentally letting go of your tent when setting it up and losing it forever to 70-mile-per-hour winds—can cost you your life.

Yet because of their intense focus, Bancroft and Arnesen not only survived but made it across Antarctica's land mass, though only part of it's ocean-covering ice shelf before the Antarctic fall forced them to call it quits. Despite failing to reach their goal, they inspired millions of people worldwide, including schoolchildren, and have gone on to more adventures, including a 2005 attempt to ski and *swim* across the polar ice cap. To me, these extraordinarily courageous, clear-headed, resourceful women exhibit most, if not all of Maslow's traits of superior human beings. They're included here because they have experienced events in their lives that fit Abraham Maslow's description of transcendent, or what he called "peak experiences." And they appear to have these experiences far more frequently than most of us.

I had the privilege of being with these two in the summer of 2000. As they trained for their Antarctica expedition, they spoke candidly about their adventures—including the peak experiences they have trekking across the ice.

"It is absolutely exhilarating," Bancroft said.

> I have the opportunity and the privilege to be in a place and be doing an activity that totally pulls everything out. I say this with some hesitation because it sounds pretty dramatic, but I almost don't care what's going on in the world. You become almost insular in your isolation. It's survival racing. You're thinking about things, but you're not going from one

thing to another. There's no clutter in your head. Everything falls into place in such a profound way.

And this is the exhilarating part—the clattering, the chatter, the extraneous noise is gone. It's so completely gone that you become in your own world. But it's an experience that most people do not ever have in this life. And to me, that's the mind-blowing part—that we don't have that available to us anymore. Very few people that I come in contact with know how to just go out and sit and be with themselves without a television, a record player, a CD . . . without the phone ringing, the beeper going off. We're bringing a lot of technology with us, and it's fabulous—I love it as much as the next person. But I love throwing myself into these places where I don't need it and I don't have it and it's turned off. It's *fabulous!*

Sometimes it's as wild and simple as skiing along. Liv and I do not talk much during the day when single-file. Facemask is on, the wind is howling. It's a very solitary kind of experience most of the time, even though we're together. It's totally being alone.[1]

Human beings are rarely alone or outdoors for any length of time anymore. We're crowded into cities of enormous scale—a far cry from the farms, villages, and small towns that populate our fairy tales and myths.

We also live interior and highly mechanized lives, relying on machines to do our work, prepare our food, regulate our climates, take us places, and protect us. Arnesen and Bancroft find that on the ice, relying on their bodies and wits for survival, they return to a self-reliance, a self-sufficiency that makes true autonomy physically real. "After so many years of doing this," Bancroft said, "what I have noticed is I don't miss much anymore. Even though these trips are so long, there's so much joy in them. We like this way of life. It's both complexity and simplicity all at once. When I was younger, I would tell you, 'Give me a salad or a shower,' but I don't even have those lists anymore. We are allowed to live in the moment."[2]

Arnesen agreed. "I don't miss anything when I am out there, because I know I have chosen to be there for a hundred days. If I miss something so much, why should I go?"[3]

What Bancroft and Arnesen get to experience are relatively frequent episodes of intense joy, calm, and unity with nature—a moment and sensation that Maslow would call a "peak experience." These are moments where the women transcend—or surpass some physical limit but also one of the mind or spirit. These moments often produce a sublime sense of unification with their natural surroundings. They usually result in a sense of effortlessness. There's almost always a suspension in the sense of time. And there are times that they even produce supernatural powers of memory.

Once while Bancroft was cross-country skiing, a movie popped into her head. It was *The Abyss*, a movie that she had seen years before. To her own amazement, she was able to play the movie in her mind from the opening title to the end credits, including every word of dialogue.

"Now, I can't remember that kind of stuff *ever!*" Bancroft admitted. "That was the clutter being gone. That's after fifty-some days of skiing and *being in my head*. I went through the whole movie several times as I'm skiing, and I didn't think of anything else. It was marvelous."[4]

In this chapter, we'll discuss how exceptional individuals share this capacity for surpassing or transcending even their own higher standards of performance and being—moments when they act effortlessly, feel great joy, lose track of time, even sense other dimensions, and are forever changed. You have probably experienced something similar at some point in your life. It may have happened in nature, in a sport, observing great art, in lovemaking, or at the end of some grueling test of endurance. Maslow found that the best among us are privileged to have more of these moments.

Maslow's Take

Abraham Maslow had a lot to say about transcendent experiences. He believed that those of us who are the healthiest psychologically are prone to having "feelings of limitless horizons opening up to the vision, the feeling of being simultaneously more powerful and also more helpless than one ever was before, the feeling of great ecstasy and wonder and awe, the loss of placing in time and space with, finally, the conviction that something extremely important and valuable had happened so that the subject is to some extent transformed and strengthened in daily life."[5]

In other words, a transcendent moment is one of rapture. It's an ecstatic sliver of exquisite calm and focus where time seems to stand still. Top athletes often describe this experience as being "in the zone." Performing artists report similar sensations. It's when everything seems to work in perfect harmony—the winning moment of a game, the sublime performance, the focused finish of some great effort. For most of us, these experiences happen less frequently and less intensely.

For Maslow and mystics throughout the ages, these moments tend to be uplifting and ego-transcending. They release creative energies and affirm the meaning and value of existence, giving people a sense of purpose—a feeling of integration with a greater whole that leaves a permanent mark, changing them for the better. These experiences can be therapeutic in that they tend to increase the individual's free will, self-determination, creativity, and empathy.

Someone having a transcendent or peak experience "not only to the world but also he himself becomes more a unity, more integrated, and self-consistent. This is another way of saying that he becomes more completely himself, idiosyncratic, unique. And since he is so, he can be more easily expressive and spontaneous without effort. All his powers then come together in their most efficient integration and coordination, organized and coordinated much more perfectly than usual."[6]

When a person is having such an experience, the individual in all sorts of ways excels at what he or she does. Rachel Walton, whom you met earlier in the book, is a hospice nurse. As she works with those who have reached the end of their lives, she also has regular experiences of intense calm, elation, and a sense that some kind of invisible hand is at work: "I feel settled in myself when I'm with these people. I have experiences where words and thoughts come through me, that I don't consciously think. I'm in the stream of something . . . I have moments of absolute joy—I think, 'It's so amazing that I get to be here with these people at this moment,' and my heart gets so *huge*."[7]

Another interesting facet of peak experiences is the effortlessness that comes with them. Maslow wrote, "Inhibition, doubt, control, self-criticism, diminish toward a zero point and he becomes the spontaneous, coordinated, efficient organism, functioning like an animal without conflict or split, without hesitation or doubt, in a great flow of power that is so peculiarly effortless, that it may become like play, masterful, virtuoso-like."[8] Rachel Walton puts it this way: "I'm not worried about whether I'm doing the right or wrong thing . . . no thought to it, it's effortless."

Many people try to recreate this kind of experience with alcohol or some other mind-altering substance. When high, they feel closer to the people they're with, even if those people are strangers. Strong individuals prefer reality and the work it takes to have genuine peak experiences.

Damian Smith as Iago

You don't have to go to the polar icecaps to have a peak experience. Back in more temperate climes, Damian Smith has experienced similar moments of ecstasy and preternatural skill. For Damian, it happens onstage.

Damian is a principal dancer with the San Francisco Ballet. A top-flight artist, his discipline has put him in the path of more peak experiences than the average person. He tells of one particularly demanding performance in the winter of 1999. He was playing Iago, Shakespeare's evil manipulator, in the ballet *Othello*. Iago corrupts the mind of King Othello, manipulating him to murder his own wife, Desdemona.

Damian became so engrossed, during one particular performance he continued to feel Iago within him. The power, the cunning, and the malevolence that Iago felt, Damian felt. It was overwhelming and frightening because not only did it feel natural, it felt *good*. Even during intermission, Damian felt removed from the dancers and stagehands around him, and he also felt disdain, as Iago would, for them.

Then, in the very last scene, Othello, Desdemona, and Iago's mistress, Amelia, lie dead on the stage. Only Iago stands, held by the king's guards. In that moment, Damian felt as if *he* was being arrested. After a long, dramatic silence, the curtain fell and the audience erupted in a roar of approval. Damian was startled: "Not until then did I remember there was an audience at all!"[9]

Damian was so permanently affected by the experience that even though "I snapped back into reality, I was not the same. Something had changed. I had changed. Experiencing something like that changes you . . . you have a deeper sense of emotion, how you look at things. Things become less literal. There are more layers around you . . . there's potentially more around you than what you're seeing."[10]

Four years later, Damian had another but quite different peak experience in Edinburgh, Scotland, at the International Arts Festival in 2003. Up to that point, his trip had been an ongoing struggle with illness, poor accommodations, and lifeless rehearsals. But on the day of the performance, Damian, his partner Julie Diana, and the San Francisco Ballet had one of those sublime moments that make for mesmerizing art.

He remembers that he and Julie lost all sense of time and space as well as the others around them. When the performance ended, they were jolted back to reality by the applause. They were so caught up in the moment that they'd actually forgotten that there was an audience.

Once again, Damian's peak experience went hand in hand with a peak performance—one that was confirmed and rewarded by an external source. The company won the coveted Festival Prize, an award that is handed out to the best performance of the entire festival.

Peak experiences are not uncommon for performing artists in front of huge audiences. But what about Rachel Walton's experiences as a nurse to the bereft and dying? Those couldn't be quieter, humbler, or more private moments. Nonetheless, the descriptions are very similar: an effortlessness, a subsuming of one's self in something greater, a suspension of time, and, most of all rapture.

Athletes Also Describe These Peak Experiences

The handsome Spanish bullfighter Gaetano Ordonyez was profiled on CBS's *60 Minutes* and was asked why he regularly risks his life in the bullring. "You kind of have a connection, a conversation with gestures, with time, with movement. You kind of lose reality and you don't care anymore about your physical existence." Were these moments of ecstasy? he was asked. "Yes, absolutely!"[11]

For Bill Bradley, peak experiences surfaced on the basketball court. In fact, they used to occur at regular intervals.

"It would be many different ways," the former NBA champion told me, "but it would be a coming together of the skills of the team in a way so that what happened was beautiful and fulfilling at the same time it succeeded. When you dribble toward someone, you see the defense playing a little bit the other way. You look at the eye of the other person; the person acknowledges what he's going to do. He goes that way, you get him the ball, he has it—about that much room for the ball to get through—he gets it right there, and he puts it in the basket. That's a moment of transporting enthusiasm. And it's a peak moment. That is the peak moment within the game."[12]

According to Bradley, when a moment like that occurs on the court, there's "a oneness about yourself and what transpired, and it's unlike anything else. It carries you to another level, and it gives you a sense of tremendous accomplishment . . . and at the same time a kind of subtle awareness that it's going to pass, so enjoy it while it's there and try to make it happen again."[13]

So how do you try to make it happen again? How do you reproduce the magic of the peak moment?

"It comes from all of this work," Bradley said, "this discipline, this build of this talent. It comes from the selflessness of saying that you're part of a team and living that. And it comes from the artistry of recognizing the moment and acting in a way that results in the desired goal: a basket."[14]

The question to ask yourself is: how can you recreate the same circumstances in your life? What is the "basket" you'd like to achieve? You don't have to be in a concert hall in Edinburgh or on the free throw line in a championship game to experience the same sort of magic—it can take place just as easily in nature. But to have a life where you regularly have peak experiences, you will likely have to devote yourself to some great or good cause.

I believe that we're all meant to live lives of consequence, or as Joseph Campbell defined a "hero," we're meant to give our lives "to something bigger" than ourselves. It's not just nice or good to be in service to great causes; it's fitting and rewarding.

The best individuals point the rest of us in the right direction not only with words or laws, but with their examples—the way they treat and love others, enjoy life, and serve the world. Their noble means are also their ends.

And that's where my life purpose comes into play. I hesitate to write this because it's so personal, but I've always felt like a messenger, and I know that this is at least one message I'm meant to deliver: you can learn from the most admirable, creative, and joyous people, you can identify them through these nineteen traits, and you can improve your life dramatically if you do so.

You have a lot of control over who you are and where you're headed.

Believe William James when he wrote, "That man has but to obey himself—He who will rest in what he is, is part of Destiny."[15] Believe Joseph Campbell, Andrew Weil, Ann Bancroft and Liv Arnesen, Jim Barksdale, Rachel Walton, Bill Bradley, Charles Schwab, Poosie Orr, and so many other wondrous, wise, and giving individuals. Let their stories energize you and educate you in their ways. In doing so, you will spot these traits and bring them into your life. They will rub off on you and you will grow richer, kinder, wiser, and happier. And as so many great philosophers and mystics have whispered through the centuries, you may even be supported by unseen forces.

Takeaways

If you learn and adopt more of the eighteen other traits described in this book you will have more transcendent or peak experiences. These are the payoff or reward for being stronger, healthier psychologically.

- ✓ Get outdoors! You don't have to ski across Antarctica to have sensory experiences that put you on a path of more transcendent experiences.

- ✓ Train and exhaust yourself physically.

- ✓ As the Reverend R. Maurice Boyd use to say, "Do your work, do your work!" The discipline and skill you develop will open doors to more peak experiences.[16]

- ✓ See a stage production of *Billy Elliot* and listen for the song, "Electricity." Find ways to "feel the fire" in the choices you make and the actions you take.

- ✓ If you don't know who you're meant to be or what path you ought to follow, retreat on your own for a time without distraction. Take the time to be still and listen to that small voice deep within you.

- ✓ Step up and perform those tasks that touch others. By being present and focused on helping those in need you can be more open and your heart more filled with joy.

Meryl Streep: Someone Who Embodies All 19 Traits

IN THIS BOOK, WE'VE met a number of exceptional human beings, from Abraham Lincoln to Mary Cunningham. These individuals stand out from the pack. Some were or are prominent leaders; others quietly contribute so much of themselves to their families and communities. Each exemplifies at least one of Abraham Maslow's nineteen traits of people who are enjoying their full potential. Actually, nearly all of them exhibit most of the traits. As I've noted, these personality characteristics flow into and support each other. But you may be wondering, do any of these characters exhibit all the traits?

We first encountered Meryl Streep in chapter 5, where we discussed the cult of celebrity—and why and how she avoids it. But it isn't just Streep's desire for privacy that sets her apart. While the media is mostly interested in her performances and box office clout, for our purposes the far more interesting story is how and why she exhibits every one of the nineteen traits.

Autonomous

Speaking at a Vassar College commencement ceremony in 1983, Streep showcased her confidence, independence, and autonomy (chapter 1). "What I'm telling you," she told graduates, "is that it goes so fast, and gets complicated so quickly, that remembering who you are and how you got there and what you really, really care about takes a hard and frequent shake-up effort."[1]

In the years since, Streep has never shied away from making that shake-up effort in her own life. Despite her many accolades, she hasn't forgotten who she is. She was once asked by *Atlanta Journal-Constitution* reporter Steve Murray, "Who is Meryl Streep?" to which she replied, "It's me. People who know me don't have to ask that. And people who don't know me are not gonna find out in a three-minute answer."[2]

Loving

Streep has also demonstrated her ability for lasting love in deep interpersonal relationships (chapter 2). Her marriage to sculptor Don Gummer is considered one of the most successful marriages in show business. The two have been married since 1978—the equivalent of ten relationships on the typical celebrity timeline.

When Laura Winters asked her the secret to such a long-lived marriage in the 2002 issue of *Vogue*, Streep replied: "Goodwill and willingness to bend—and to shut up every once in a while. There's no road map on how to raise a family: it's always an enormous negotiation. But I have a holistic need to work and to have huge ties of love in my life. I can't imagine eschewing one for the other."[3]

Streep also maintains close relationships with her family. At the 2010 Golden Globe Awards Ceremony, where she was nominated twice for best actress and won for her portrayal of Julia Child in *Julie and Julia*, she gave the following tribute to her mother:

> I just want to say that in my long career, I've played so many extraordinary women that I'm being mistaken for one. No, really, I'm very clear that I'm a vessel for other people's stories and other women's lives. And this year, I got to play not only one of the most beloved women in America—Julia Child. But, I also got to secretly pay homage to my own personal, not so famous hero. That's my mother. Who was of the same generation as Julia. Who shared her verve. A lot of the people in this room knew my mother and knew that she had a real joy in living. And she just had no patience for gloom and doom. I'm not like that. I come to Golden Globes weekend and I'm really, honestly conflicted how to have my happy movie self in the face of everything that I'm aware of in the real world. That's when I have my mother's voice coming to me saying, "Partners in health, shoot some money to partners in health, put the dress on, put on a smile and be damn grateful that you can have the dollars to help and have the next day, and the next day and the next day." I *am* really grateful. I am really grateful![4]

People within her extended family also report that Streep is always "normal" and a wonderful aunt and family member to everyone. That's worth all the Hollywood accolades to me.

Ethical

Streep's persona, which we see in certain roles and in interviews, is the same personality that she has at home—making her an integrated human being. And she is self-aware and wise enough to know the value of integration and integrity (chapter 3).

In her 1983 Vassar commencement speech, Streep urged graduates to "integrate what you believe into every single area of your life." Then listen to how she expands this into an urgent declaration of integrated self-determination: "Take your heart to work, and ask the most and best of everybody else too. Don't let your special character and values, the secret that you know and no one else does, the truth—don't let that get swallowed up by the great chewing complacency."[5] Aren't these the ideas of Joseph Campbell and William James and Abraham Maslow?

Unaffected

Streep didn't let celebrity change her, and she hasn't let the "great chewing complacency" of casting directors pigeonhole her. The actor who seemed perfect for only tragic roles after Oscar-winning performances in *Kramer vs. Kramer* and *Sophie's Choice* then wowed us with her comedic talents in *Mamma Mia!* and *Julie & Julia*. Despite her early status as a wounded and sympathetic icon, she did an excellent job of resisting what others thought she was capable of. On a personal basis she resists ads, fads, and fashion, declaring more than once that she was *not* wearing some new designer gown (chapter 4).

While many actresses shape themselves into what others want, Streep has brilliantly resisted the media zeitgeist. She's even flown directly in the face of major sponsors. At a gathering of women business leaders in 1999, Streep described her experience with the marketers of the movie *The River Wild*. "The real queasy moments came in the marketing meeting, when I made big enemies because I wouldn't approve the use of my big face on the poster pointing a pistol at America. The N.R.A., rich as it is, doesn't have the money or the clout to get glamorous actors of such renown to pose for their ads. But we do their flogging for free every time we point the gun at the camera for an ad campaign."[6]

Private

We've already discussed how Streep fiercely protects her privacy (chapter 5) and in her own snappy retort, "I don't think it helps the suspension of disbelief if everybody knows where you work out." She "hates" having her picture taken and she shields her family from the media. When asked about the fact that a lot of people don't know that she has four children, she replied, "Well, they're not photographed and celebrated as my appendages, no."[7]

Detached

The woman who has given us so many memorable performances is keenly objective, even detached about herself, her work (as "a vessel" for others' stories), and her public image (chapter 6). No self-absorbed star here. "Your reputation is something that you carry with you and it gets in the way maybe the first five minutes of meeting people or beginning a project," Streep said. "It's a thing that stands apart from who you are and how you relate. But with the exigencies of movie-making, it all goes away as you act together."[8]

She also suggested that people "put blinders on to those things that conspire to hold you back, especially the ones in your own head." Here, Streep is advocating a transcendence of self that has served her well over the years. Of all the photos included in the 2010 *Vanity Fair* cover story, her favorite shot of herself is the one where she has no makeup, no artifice. She's looking frankly at the camera with a generous, unforced smile. As she described it, that is the one picture where "they scraped all the crap off my face!"[9]

Experiential

When it comes to being open to experience, you can't get more open than Streep (chapter 7). She recalls telling her agent,

"I've got to do something outside of Manhattan, outside of 1981, outside of my experience. Put me on the moon. I want to be some-place else. I want to be held in the boundaries of a different time and place."[10] The roles that followed—leads in *The French Lieu-tenant's Woman* and *Sophie's Choice*—cemented her reputation as cinema's leading lady and garnered her a second Academy Award.

Realistic

Despite her desire to be swept up in another time and place, Streep has never sacrificed her clear perception of reality (chapter 8). Like all very healthy psyches, she sees everything with less baggage and in a penetrating way. John Patrick Shanley, who wrote the play *Doubt* (Streep starred in the film adaptation), noted in the *Vanity Fair* article, "On one level, she is just like a big mischievous cat—like a cat who sits in the corner and watches everyone and her tail twitches. She's going inward and assessing outward."[11]

In other words, Streep is a great observer. She sees reality better and with less effort than most of us. Her freshness of perception allows her to deftly capture the human experience and helps her convey it in the characters she portrays.

Laid Back

Shanley also describes Streep as someone who is "completely open to free association . . . and she doesn't assume she knows the answer."[12] She's humble and quite fine simply not knowing. This indicates a certain, if not high level of serenity in the face of mystery or the unknown (chapter 9).

Performance and Process Oriented

Streep's approach to acting is a testament to the fact that she's not merely performance oriented; like the great ballerina Muriel Maffre, Streep is interested in the process too (chapter 10). As she told the Vassar class of 1983, "There's always the knowledge that the work itself is the reward, and if I choose challenging work, it'll pay me back with interest. At least I'll be interested, even if nobody else is. That choice, between the devil and the dream, comes up every day in different little disguises. I'm sure it comes up in every field of endeavor and every life.

"My advice is to look the dilemma in the face and decide what you can live with . . . I firmly believe that this engagement in the attempt for excellence is what sustains the most well-lived and satisfying, successful lives."[13]

Egalitarian

This excellence translates into doing tangible good for the world. Instead of putting herself up on a pedestal, Streep considers herself right there beside us, fighting in the trenches. Her egalitarian outlook not only gives her humility but also gives her added responsibility as just another "citizen of the earth" (chapter 11).

As she put it, "As my network expands and my responsibilities multiply, so does my own stake in the future of the world, and instead of feeling the desire to keep quiet, I feel the need to demand the best of our leaders, to secure the quality of the life my children will live into the next century, to secure the FACT of their survival into the next century. In other words . . . I must obey this incentive to excellence—not just in making a scene work, but in making The Scene, in participating fully and taking on the responsibilities we all share as citizens of the earth."[14]

Jolly

Despite her dedication to weighty causes, Streep is certainly no stranger to lighthearted laughter (chapter 12). At Yale Repertory Theater, she played a wizened, crippled old crone in *The Idiots Karamazov*—even though she was only in her twenties at the time. It was her debut into comedic roles, and eventually it led to many more. People describe her sense of humor as effervescent. It's certainly never caustic or cruel. And, like all healthy people, she loves comedy. Many years ago, when asked what dream role she had always wanted to play, she replied, "To be in something that people are laughing so hard that it hurts, you know?"[15]

Empathic

Perhaps the reason Meryl Streep is such a brilliant actor is that she has profound empathy for human beings and an ability to deeply identify with all humanity (chapter 13). In telling *Cosmopolitan* magazine about her character choices, she said, "The great gift of human beings is that we have the power of empathy. We can all sense a mysterious connection to each other. I like to investigate these different women to see what their commonality is with me. When I get the script and read their story, I hear the 'ping!' that makes a connection with my own life."[16]

At a 2006 speech given for the What Women Want gathering hosted by *Marie Claire* in New York City, Streep stated, "I've thought a lot about the power of empathy. In my work, it's the current that connects me and my actual pulse to a fictional character in a made-up story. It allows me to feel pretend feelings and sorrows and imagined pain. And my nervous system is sympathetically wired, and it conducts that current to you, sitting in a movie theatre.

"I used to wonder, 'Why and how did we evolve with this weak and useless passion intact within the deep heart's core?' And the answer I've formulated to myself is that empathy is the engine that powers all the best in us. It is what civilizes us." [17]

Dutiful

Streep's empathy is not merely professional. She doesn't close up shop at the end of a long day at the studio and return to a cloistered, self-focused world. On the contrary: she is incredibly responsible and problem focused (chapter 14). She supports a number of causes, including the fight against AIDS, help for at-risk and disadvantaged youth, cancer research, hunger relief, and human rights. She has supported charities from Artists for Peace and Justice to Healthy Child Healthy World.

Streep is outspoken in her frustration over the peculiarly American notion that nobody cares about celebrities' opinions on world events. Because she herself is so integrated, she considers it normal that her responsibilities extend beyond the silver screen. When asked about her experiences with journalists, she stated,

> The questions are basically the same on both sides of the Atlantic, with one startling difference.
>
> In Europe, as a matter of course, along with, "How do you manage to combine family and career?" and "How does your husband handle your success?" and "How do you pick your scripts?" and "What is your real hair color?" there would inevitably be a category of questions on the state of the world. It was just assumed, without any embarrassment at all, that as a member of the human race I had one or two thoughts on the subject—this from Swedes and Spaniards, Italians, Germans, English and French . . . everybody! Everybody but the home team . . . Now why is that? The American journalists never ask you that, or, if they do, they invariably make some crack about Jane Fonda. [18]

In Streep's mind—her duties, indeed, all of our duties—extend well beyond one's personal sphere. Her celebrity status is all the *more* reason to contribute to bigger issues, as opposed to focusing solely on her own, limited existence.

Appreciative

There's no denying that Streep exhibits a classic freshness of appreciation. You can *feel* it every time she gives an award acceptance speech (chapter 15). Mike Nichols, who has directed Streep four times, said that you can feel her excitement at each new day on the set. In the *Vanity Fair* cover story, the actress described how grateful she is just to be alive. "I have so many friends who are sick or gone, and I'm here. Are you kidding? No complaints!"[19]

Creative

Streep appears to have never lost her creativity and thus she's not had to recover it. She is widely considered to be the best actress of the modern era, enough said (chapter 16).

Exuberant

Streep is also spontaneous and expressive—a woman who feels deeply and isn't afraid to show the depths of her emotions (chapter 17). "I want to feel my life while I'm in it," she said.[20] She embraces Bill Bradley's idea that "feeling is as important as thinking." When asked what advice she had for a young aspiring actress, she said, "Get a good education, know as much as you can about everything, and listen. Look at the world—you know—*feelingly.*" For Streep, that expressiveness more often than not becomes sheer exuberance.

Joyous

Is it any wonder that, with this love for creative and spontaneous expression, Streep derives passionate joy from her art? She's got a real zest for living and working (chapter 18). In each role she takes on, she looks "for the thing that I got from it from the beginning. Because that's the thing that intoxicates me . . . You feel it in pivotal moments in your life: when someone is born, when you fall in love, when someone dies, when someone tells a great joke and you haven't laughed in a week and you just howl. The top flies off of your head. That's what you look for. And that's what happens in acting all the time."[21]

This happiness spills over into Streep's day-to-day life too. "Guard your good mood," she advised. "Listen to music every day, joke, and love, and read more for fun—especially poetry."[22]

Transcendent

Like all exceptional people, Streep seems to have more transcendent experiences—those sublime moments where one feels unity with nature or one's surroundings and a sense that one has changed (chapter 19). Her first "acting epiphany" happened in college. "I was in *Miss Julie*, a Strindberg play . . . there was a moment where you leave everything behind—transcendence or something. It's another state, definitely. And it's great. It's like when I used to swim and there was a point where you just fly. I always go in search of that."[23]

Meryl Streep isn't just one of the best actors of our generation. She's one of the best human beings.

Let Them Rub Off on You

Sad to say, most of us probably won't have the opportunity to spend time with Meryl Streep anytime soon. But if Maslow is right and people as strong, wise, generous, and fun as Streep really do make up 1 percent of the population, then there are three million of them in America alone. Be on the lookout for the Meryl Streeps, Andrew Fergusons, Rachel Waltons, and Poosie Orrs in your life. Bring them into your orbit—your work, your play, and best of all, your family. They can't help but rub off on you!

Notes

Preface

1. Leo Tolstoy, *Anna Karenina* (Hertfordshire: Wordsworth Editions Limited, 1995), 1.

Introduction

1. Dr. Stephen R. Covey, interview by author, *Great Leaders*, Episode 114, KTVS, Detroit Public Television, 2001.

Chapter 1

1. Andrew Weil, interview by author, *Great Leaders*, WTVS, Detroit Public Television, 2002.

2. Abraham Maslow, *Motivation and Personality*, 3rd ed. (New York: Addison-Wesley, 1987), 134.

3. William James, *In the Maelstrom of American Modernism* (New York: Houghton-Mifflin, 2007), 202.

4. Maslow, *Motivation and Personality*, 135.

5. Ibid., 136.

6. Charles T. Munger, *Poor Charlie's Almanack: The Wit and Wisdom of Charles Munger* (Virginia Beach: PCA Publications, LLC, 2005), 15.

7. Maslow, *Motivation and Personality*, 130.

8. Ibid., 131.

9. Rev. R. Maurice Boyd, interview by author, July 1998, New York, NY.

10. Jim Barksdale, interview by author, *Nightly Business Report*, "Prime Movers," WPBT Television, September 2000.

11. John M. Maher and Dennie Briggs, eds., *An Open Life: Joseph Campbell in Conversation with Michael Toms* (New York: Larson Publications, 1988), 107.

12. Jack Welch, interview by author, *Great Leaders,* Episode 5, "Sumner Redstone and Jack Welch," KTVS, Detroit Public Television, 2001.

13. Bill Bradley, interview by author, 2002, San Francisco, CA.

14. Friedrich Nietzsche, *Thus Spoke Zarathustra: A Book for All and None* (Cambridge: Cambridge University Press, 2006), Appendixes, 10.

15. James, *American Modernism,* 181.

16. *Shorter Oxford English Dictionary,* 3rd ed., s.v. "Wise."

17. Maslow, *Motivation and Personality,* 157.

18. James, *American Modernism,* 203.

19. Boyd, interview.

20. Ibid.

21. J. K. Rowling, *Harry Potter and the Chamber of Secrets* (New York: Scholastic, 1999), 333.

22. Barksdale, interview; Bradley, interview; Weil, interview; Welch, interview; James, *American Modernism,* 203.

Chapter 2

1. Paula Orr, interview by author, April 9, 2010, Pittsburgh, PA.

2. Ibid.

3. Ibid.

4. Ibid.

5. Ibid.

6. Ibid.

7. Maslow, *Motivation and Personality,* 157.

8. Orr, interview.

9. Ibid.

10. Maslow, *Motivation and Personality,* 153.

11. Ibid.

12. Jodi Kantor, "Obama's Friends Form Strategy to Stay Close," *New York Times,* December 13, 2008, Politics section, http://www.nytimescom/2008/12/14/us/politics/14friends.html.

13. Maslow, *Motivation and Personality,* 152.

14. Rachel Walton, interview by author, March 2010.

15. Mrs. John F. Walton Jr., interview by author, August 1998, Ontario, Canada.

16. R. Walton, interview.

17. Ibid.

18. Ibid.

19. Ibid.

20. Maslow, *Motivation and Personality,* 129.

21. R. Walton, interview.

22. Ibid.

23. Orr, interview.

24. Ibid.

25. Ibid.

26. Maslow, *Motivation and Personality*, 152.

27. Orr, interview.

28. Maslow, *Motivation and Personality*, 133.

29. Ibid., 131.

Chapter 3

1. Associated Press, "Enron Whistleblower Tells of 'Crooked Company,'" *msnbc.com,* March 15, 2006, http://www.msnbc.msn.com/id/11839694.

2. Ibid.

3. Ibid.

4. Ibid.

5. Maslow, *Motivation and Personality*, 141.

6. Abraham Maslow, *The Farther Reaches of Human Nature* (New York: Penguin Arcana, 1993), 44.

7. Boyd, interview.

8. Maslow, *Motivation and Personality*, 141.

9. Warren Buffett and Charles Munger, interview by author, *Moneyline*, May 1993.

10. Wesco, "Notes on the Wesco Financial Annual Meeting," May 6, 2009, http://www.rbcpa.com/wesco_notes_Annual_Meeting_2009.pdf.

11. Ibid.

12. James Armstrong, interview by author, December 2009.

13. "Wesco Meeting."

14. Ibid.

15. Ibid.

16. Alice Schroeder, *The Snowball: Warren Buffet and the Business of Life* (New York: Bantam Dell, 2008), 826.

17. *Shorter Oxford English Dictionary*, 3rd ed., s.v. "Authentic."

18. Covey, interview.

Chapter 4

1. Joyce Wadler, "At Home with: Dr. Andrew Weil; What Goes with Gray?" *New York Times,* October 20, 2005, http://query.nytimes.com/gst/fullpage.html?res=9C05EFDD123FF933A15753C1A9639C8B63&pagewanted=2.

2. Maslow, *Motivation and Personality*, 133.

3. Weil, interview.

4. Maslow, *Motivation and Personality*, 135.

5. Ibid., 132.

6. Walter Isaacson, *Einstein: His Life and Universe* (New York: Simon & Schuster, 2007), 159.

7. Maslow, *Motivation and Personality*, 145.

8. *Lawrence of Arabia,* directed by David Lean (1963; London, England: Horizon Pictures Ltd.).

9. Maslow, *Motivation and Personality*, 135.

10. Robert M. Higdon, interview by author, 1995.

11. Ibid.

Chapter 5

1. Bradley, interview.

2. Brad Goldfarb, "Meryl Streep: Facing the Myths with the World's Number One Actor's Actor," *Interview,* December 2002, 150.

3. Maslow, *Motivation and Personality*, 134.

4. Ibid., 136.

5. Isaacson, *Einstein: His Life and Universe*, 274.

6. Jim Collins, *Good to Great: Why Some Companies Make the Leap . . . and Others Don't* (New York: HarperBusiness, 2001), 33.

7. Leslie Bennetts, "Something about Meryl," *Vanity Fair*, January 2010.

8. Ibid.

Chapter 6

1. Mary Cunningham is not her real name. Her name as well as those of her family members have been changed to protect their privacy.

2. Cathy and Melinda Cunningham, interview by author, February 2010.

3. Ibid.

4. Ibid.

5. Ibid.

6. Ibid.

7. Ibid.

8. Mary Cunningham, interview by author, November 2008, Ojai, CA.

9. Maslow, *Motivation and Personality*, 136.

10. Ibid.

11. Ibid.

12. Ibid.

13. Maslow, *Motivation and Personality*, 134.

14. *Star Wars: Episode VI—Return of the Jedi*, directed by Richard Marquand (Los Angeles: 20th Century Fox, 1983).

15. Maslow, *Motivation and Personality*, 134.

16. Weil, interview.

17. Covey, interview.

18. Andrew Weil, interview by author, February 2010.

19. Cathy and Melinda Cunningham, interview.

Chapter 7

1. Sabeer Bahtia, interview by author, "Prime Movers," *Nightly Business Report*, 2001.

2. Ibid.

3. Andy H., "Warren Buffett Speaks: 25 Best Warren Buffett Quotes on His Strategies, Investments, and Cheap Suits," *Bankling.com*, May 7, 2009.

4. Maslow, *Motivation and Personality*, 139.

5. Bradley, interview.

6. Joseph Campbell, interview by Bill Moyers, *The Power of Myth*, PBS, 1988.

7. *Shorter Oxford English Dictionary*, 3rd ed., s.v. "Rapture."

8. James, *American Modernism*, 207.

Chapter 8

1. Dan Case, interview by author, *Great Entrepreneurs,* Episode 105, WPBT, 2001.

2. Steve Case, interview by author, *Great Entrepreneurs*, Episode 105, WPBT, 2001.

3. Kara Swisher, interview by author, *Great Entrepreneurs*, Episode 105, WPBT, 2001.

4. Maslow, *Motivation and Personality*, 143.

5. Andy Grove, interview by author, *Great Entrepreneurs*, Episode 110, WPBT, 2001.

6. Natalie Angier, "Finally, the Spleen Gets Some Respect," *New York Times*, August 3, 2009, http://www.nytimes.com/2009/08/04/science/04angier.html.

7. Maslow, *Motivation and Personality*, 128.

8. Ibid., 129.

9. Ibid.

10. Munger, *Poor Charlie's Almanack*, 55.

11. Ibid., 15.

12. Ibid., 80.

13. M. Scott Peck, *The Road Less Traveled*, 2nd ed. (New York: Touchstone, 1998), 50.

14. Ibid., 45.

15. Maslow, *Motivation and Personality*, 129.

16. Ibid.

17. Meryl Streep, interview by James Lipton, Inside the Actors Studio, quoted in Creative Artists Agency, "Meryl Streep in Her Own Words," Meryl Streep Online, http://www.merylstreeponline.net.

18. Shelly Lazarus, interview by author, February 2010, New York, NY.

19. Maslow, *Motivation and Personality*, 147.

Chapter 9

1. Melinda Cunningham, interview by author, August 1998.

2. Ibid.

3. Ibid.

4. Maslow, Motivation and Personality, 134.

5. Ibid., 130.

6. Ibid,, 134.

7. Melinda Cunningham, interview.

8. Maslow, *Motivation and Personality*, 130.

9. Ibid.

10. Melinda Cunningham, interview.

11. Ibid.

12. Maslow, *Motivation and Personality*, 130.

13. Ibid.

14. Ibid., 134.

Chapter 10

1. Muriel Maffre, interview by author, May 2010, San Francisco, CA.

2. Ibid.

3. Ibid.

4. Damian Smith, interview by author, May 2010, San Francisco, CA.

5. Maffre interview, May 2010.

6. Ibid.

7. Ibid.

8. Ibid.

9. Ibid.

10. Ibid.

11. Maslow, *Motivation and Personality*, 149.

12. Ibid.

13. Ibid., 141.

14. Ibid., 122.

15. Ibid., 126.

16. Pelikan, "Full Text: Warren Buffet Letter to Berkshire Hathaway Shareholders," February, 2009, Clips and Comment, February 28, 2009, http://www.clipsandcomment.com/2009/02/28/full-text-warren-buffet-letter-to-berkshire-hathaway-shareholders-february-2009/.

17. February 8, 2009, http://www.pbs.org/moyers/faithandreason/perspectives1.htm.

18. Weil, interview, 2002.

19. Marleen McDaniel, interview by author, *Nightly Business Report*, WPBT, 2000.

20. Munger, *Poor Charlie's Almanack*, 162.

21. Maslow, *Motivation and Personality*, 141.

Chapter 11

1. Andrew Ferguson, interview by author, April 9, 2010, Pittsburgh, PA.

2. Ibid.

3. Ibid.

4. Ibid.

5. Ibid.

6. Maslow, *Motivation and Personality*, 135.

7. Ferguson, interview.

8. Ibid.

9. Ibid.

10. Ibid.

11. Ibid.

12. Ibid.

13. Ibid.

14. Ibid.

15. Ibid.

16. Maslow, *Motivation and Personality*, 139.

17. Ibid.

18. Ferguson, interview.

19. Susan Estrich et al., "My Boss, Justice Stevens," *New York Times*, Opinion section, April 9, 2010, http://www.nytimes.com/2010/04/11/opinion/11stevens .html?pagewanted=all.

20. Doris Kearns Goodwin, *Team of Rivals* (New York: Simon & Schuster, 1995), 553.

21. Dennis Conner, interview by author, *Great Leaders*, Episode 208, WTVS, Detroit Public Television, October 2001.

Chapter 12

1. *Good Morning, Vietnam,* directed by Barry Levinson (Touchstone Pictures, 1988).

2. Maslow, *Motivation and Personality*, 141.

3. Orr, interview.

4. Goodwin, *Team of Rivals*, 588.

5. Ellen DeGeneres, *Ellen*, September 7, 2010, http://ellen.warnerbros.com/.

6. YouTube, "Ellen DeGeneres Commencement Speech at Tulane University," May 16, 2009, http://wateryourbrain.com/main/detail/50?title=Ellen+DeGeneres +Commencement+Speech+at+Tulane+University+.

7. Martha Stewart, interview by Diane Ettelson, *Great Entrepreneurs*, WPBT Television, 2001.

8. Internet Movie Data Base, "Ellen DeGeneres: Biography," http://www .imdb.com/name/nm0001122/bio.

9. Maslow, *Motivation and Personality*, 134.

10. Bill Nye, interview by Wired.com, April 2005.

Chapter 13

1. Charles Schwab Corporation, "Schwab Reports Fourth Quarter and Full Year Results," news release, January 19, 2010, http://www.aboutschwab.com/ media/pdf/q4_2009_earnings.pdf.

2. Charles Schwab, interview by author, *Great Entrepreneurs*, Episode 108, WPBT, 2001.

3. Donald T. Regan, interview by author, *Today's Business*, June 1984.

4. Schwab, interview.

5. Ibid.

6. Ibid.

7. Ibid.

8. Ibid.

9. Ibid.

10. Ibid.

11. Ibid.

12. Maslow, *Motivation and Personality*, 140.

13. Ibid., 138.

14. Ibid.

15. Ibid., 139.

16. Ibid.

17. Goodwin, *Team of Rivals*, 175.

18. Chief Seattle, "Chief Seattle's Letter," http://www.barefootsworld.net/seattle.html.

Chapter 14

1. Grove, interview.

2. Ibid.

3. Ibid.

4. Ibid.

5. Ibid.

6. Ibid.

7. Ibid.

8. Ibid.

9. Ibid.

10. Maslow, *Motivation and Personality*, 134.

11. Ibid., 138.

12. Associated Press, "Hero Pilot Tells of 'Shocking' Moment Engines Cut Out," *Sydney Morning Herald,* World section, February 4, 2009, http://www.smh.com.au/news/world/hero-pilot-tells-of-shocking-moment-engines-cut-out/2009/02/04/1233423276808.html.

13. Ibid.

14. Larry McShane, "Hero Pilot Chesley (Sully) Sullenberger and Crew of Flight 1549 Get Keys to New York City," *Daily News*, February 9, 2009, http://www.nydailynews.com/ny_local/2009/02/09/2009-02-09_hero_pilot_chesley_sully_sullenberger_an.html.

15. Alex Altman, review of *Fly by Wire: The Geese, the Glide, the Miracle on the Hudson,* by William Langewiesche, *Time,* November 19, 2009, http://www.time.com/time/arts/article/0,8599,1940508,00.html.

16. Bradley, interview.

17. Mrs. John F. Walton Jr., interview by author, Ontario, Canada, August 1998.

Chapter 15

1. Mrs. J. F. Walton Jr., interview.
2. Ibid.
3. Ibid.
4. Ibid.
5. Rachel Walton, telephone interview by author, March 2010.
6. Ibid.
7. Maslow, *Motivation and Personality*, 136.
8. Ibid., 137.
9. Ibid.
10. Campbell, interview.
11. Boyd, interview.
12. Ibid.
13. Ibid.
14. Orr, interview.
15. Ibid.
16. Ibid.
17. Ibid.

Chapter 16

1. Julia Cameron, *Floor Sample* (New York: Penguin, 2007). Kindle edition.
2. Ibid., 65.
3. Ibid., 1446–51.
4. Ibid., 1432–37.
5. Julia Cameron, "Julia Cameron Biography," *http://www.theartistsway.com/ julia-cameron*.
6. Cameron, *Floor Sample*, 1316–21.
7. Maslow, *Motivation and Personality*, 142.
8. Ibid., 143.
9. Steve Pitzel, "If You Want to Be Creative, Get Out There and Do It. It's Not a Waste of Time," Intel Software Network (blog), March 9, 2010, http:// software.intel.com/en-us/blogs/2010/03/09/if-you-want-to-be-creative-get-out-there-and-do-it-its-not-a-waste-of-time/.
10. Orr, interview.
11. Ibid.

12. Ibid.
13. Ferguson, interview.
14. Ibid.
15. R. Walton, interview.
16. Ibid.
17. Boyd, interview.
18. Campbell, interview.

Chapter 17

1. Welch, interview.
2. Ibid.
3. Ibid.
4. Maslow, *Motivation and Personality*, 160.
5. Welch, interview.
6. Welch, interview.

Chapter 18

1. Shelly Lazarus, interview by author, ManagemenTV, February 2010, Buenos Aires, Argentina.
2. Ibid.
3. Ibid.
4. Joanne Gordon, *Be Happy at Work: 100 Women Who Love Their Jobs, and Why* (New York: Ballantine Books, 2009), 73.
5. Rochelle Lazarus, "Commencement Address 2005," Smith College, May 15, 2005, http://www.smith.edu/collegerelations/com2005.php
6. Maslow, *Toward a Psychology of Being*, 3rd ed., (New York: John Wiley & Sons, 1999), 160.
7. Shelly Lazarus, Commencement address, Smeal College of Business, Pennsylvania State University, PA, May 2009.
8. Jerry Greenfield, interview by author, *Great Leaders*, WTVS, Detroit Public Television, 2002.
9. Ben Cohen, interview by author, *Great Leaders*, WTVS, Detroit Public Television, 2002.
10. Greenfield, interview.
11. Maslow, *Motivation and Personality*, 157.

Chapter 19

1. Ann Bancroft, interview by author, *Great Leaders*, WTVS, Detroit Public Television, 2000.

2. Ibid.

3. Liv Arnesen, interview by author, *Great Leaders*, WTVS, Detroit Public Television, 2000.

4. Bancroft, interview.

5. Maslow, *Motivation and Personality*, 137.

6. Ibid., 164.

7. R. Walton, interview.

8. Maslow, *Motivation and Personality*, 164.

9. Damian Smith, interview by author, May 2010, San Francisco, CA.

10. Ibid.

11. CBS, "Bullfighting's Blood Brothers," *60 Minutes*, August 19, 2009, http://www.cbsnews.com/stories/2008/10/16/60minutes/main4526581.shtml.

12. Bradley, interview.

13. Ibid.

14. Ibid.

15. James, *American Modernism*, 202.

16. Boyd, interview.

Epilogue

1. Meryl Streep, "Welcome to the Big Time," Vassar commencement speech, 1983, quoted in Creative Artists Agency, "Commencement Address," Meryl Streep Online, http://www.merylstreeponline.net/.

2. Meryl Streep, interview by Steve Murray, *Atlanta Journal-Constitution*, quoted in Creative Artists Agency, "Meryl Streep in Her Own Words," Meryl Streep Online, http://www.merylstreeponline.net/MSQ.html.

3. Meryl Streep, interview by Laura Winters, *Vogue*, December 2002, quoted in Creative Artists Agency, "Meryl Streep in Her Own Words," Meryl Streep Online, http://www.merylstreeponline.net/MSQ.html.

4. Meryl Streep, "2010 Golden Globe Awards Acceptance Speech," http://www.youtube.com/watch?v=I-iLC59tgRs.

5. Streep, "Welcome to the Big Time."

6. Meryl Streep, "Speech to Women Leaders in Communications Businesses," November 18, 1999, quoted in Creative Artists Agency, "Meryl Streep in Her Own Words," Meryl Streep Online, http://www.merylstreeponline.net/byms2.html.

7. Goldfarb, "Meryl Streep," *Interview,* December 2002, quoted in Creative Artists Agency, "Meryl Streep in Her Own Words," Meryl Streep Online, http://www.merylstreeponline.net/FAQ.html.

8. Meryl Streep, "Meryl's Choices," *Los Angeles Times,* quoted in Creative Artists Agency, "Meryl Streep in Her Own Words," Meryl Streep Online, http://www.merylstreeponline.net/MSQ.html.

9. Bennetts, "Something about Meryl."

10. Meryl Streep, quoted in Creative Artists Agency, "Artistry," Meryl Streep Online, http://www.merylstreeponline.net/work.html.

11. Bennetts, "Something about Meryl."

12. Ibid.

13. Meryl Streep, "Welcome to the Big Time."

14. Ibid.

15. Meryl Streep, interview by Ken Burns, *USA Today,* December 2010, quoted in Creative Artists Agency, "Meryl Streep in Her Own Words," Meryl Streep Online, http://www.merylstreeponline.net/MSQ.html.

16. Meryl Streep, interview by Michael Segell, *Cosmopolitan,* May 1991, quoted in Creative Artists Agency, "Meryl Streep in Her Own Words," Meryl Streep Online, http://www.merylstreeponline.net/MSQ.html.

17. Meryl Streep, "The Power of Empathy," speech given at "What Women Want" conference hosted by *Marie Claire,* May 4, 2006, New York, NY, quoted in Creative Artists Agency, "The Power of Empathy," Meryl Streep Online, http://www.merylstreeponline.net/byms5.html.

18. Meryl Streep, "Welcome to the Big Time."

19. Bennetts, "Something about Meryl."

20. Meryl Streep, interview by Ken Burns.

21. Meryl Streep, quoted in Creative Artists Agency, "Meryl Streep in Her Own Words," Meryl Streep Online, http://www.merylstreeponline.net/MSQ.html.

22. Meryl Streep, "University of New Hampshire Commencement Address," quoted in Creative Artists Agency, "Meryl Streep in Her Own Words," Meryl Streep Online, http://www.merylstreeponline.net/MSQ.html.

23. Meryl Streep, quoted in Creative Artists Agency, "Meryl Streep in Her Own Words."

Recommended Reading

Einstein: His Life and Universe. Walter Isaacson. Simon & Schuster, 2007.

Motivation and Personality. Abraham Maslow. Revised by Robert Frager, James Fadiman, Cynthia McReynolds, and Ruth Cox, Longman, 1970.

Poor Charlie's Almanack: The Wit and Wisdom of Charles T. Munger. Edited by Peter D. Kaufman. PCA Publishing, 2005.

The Road Less Traveled: A New Psychology of Love, Traditional Values and Spiritual Growth. M. Scott Peck, MD, Touchstone, 1978.

The 7 Habits of Highly Effective People: Powerful Lessons in Personal Change. Stephen R. Covey. Free Press, 2004.

"Something about Meryl." Leslie Bennetts. *Vanity Fair.* January 2010.

Team of Rivals: The Political Genius of Abraham Lincoln. Doris Kearns Goodwin. Simon & Schuster, 2005. Within the five-page introduction, Goodwin enumerates Lincoln's personal qualities that helped make him not only a great leader but also, in the words of his one-time rival and attorney general, Edward Bates, "very near a perfect man."

Index